Richard Mansfield

BEAU
BRUMMEL

A Play in Four Acts

Written for

RICHARD MANSFIELD

By

CLYDE FITCH

New York
JOHN LANE COMPANY
MCMVIII

The PERSONS of the PLAY

The Prince of Wales (Heir apparent to the throne of England)

Beau Brummel (Prince of dandies)

Richard Brinsley Sheridan (Playwright)

Reginald Courtenay (Nephew to the Beau)

Mortimer (Valet and confidential servant to the Beau)

Mr. Oliver Vincent (A self-made merchant, father of Mariana)

Lord Manly (A fop)

Mr. Abrahams (A money lender)

Bailiffs

Prince's Footman

Simpson (Footman to Beau)

The Duchess of Leamington (Middle-aged, but very anxious to appear young)

Mariana Vincent (Young and beautiful, beloved by Beau and Reginald)

Mrs. St. Aubyn (Passée but still beautiful—very anxious to captivate the Prince but unwilling to resign the Beau)

Kathleen (Irish maid of Mariana)

Lady Farthingale (Pretty—insipid)

A French Lodging-house Keeper

A Nurse

The FIRST ACT

FIRST SCENE—The morning toilet. Mr. Brummel despatches a proposal of marriage, assists his nephew, and sends for a new tailor.

SECOND SCENE—The Beau receives a number of friends and makes an unfortunate blunder.

The SECOND ACT

A small and early party at Carlton House. Mr. Brummel proposes to an heiress and reprimands a Prince.

The THIRD ACT

The Mall and how it came about that Mr. Brummel had a previous engagement with His Majesty.

The FOURTH ACT

FIRST SCENE (*six months later*)—Mr. Brummel's lodgings in Calais.

SECOND SCENE—The attic at Caen. A very poor dinner with an excellent dessert.

*T*HIS play was first produced at the Madison Square Theatre by Richard Mansfield, on May 17, 1890. The 250th representation took place at the Garden Theatre, on January 30, 1891.

The CAST *on this* OCCASION *was*

Beau Brummel	MR. RICHARD MANSFIELD
The Prince of Wales . .	MR. D. H. HARKINS
Richard Brinsley Sheridan .	MR. A. G. ANDREWS
Lord Manly	MR. H. G. LONSDALE
Reginald Courtenay . . .	MR. VINCENT STERNROYD
Mortimer	MR. W. J. FERGUSON
Mr. Abrahams	MR. HARRY GWYNETTE
Simpson	MR. SMILES
Bailiffs	MR. GWYNETTE and MR. IVAN PERONETTE
Prince's Footman . . .	MR. F. F. GRAHAM
Mr. Oliver Vincent . . .	MR. W. H. CROMPTON
Mariana Vincent . . .	MISS BEATRICE CAMERON
Kathleen	MISS ETHEL SPRAGUE
The Duchess of Leamington .	MRS. JULIA BRUTONE
Lady Farthingale	MISS HELEN GLIDDEN
French Lodging-house Keeper	MISS HAZEL SELDEN
Nurse	MISS GENEVRA CAMPBELL
Mrs. St. Aubyn	MISS ADELA MEASOR

THE FIRST ACT

SCENE ONE

BEAU BRUMMEL

THE FIRST ACT

SCENE ONE

The scene represents the BEAU'S *dressing-room. A cheerful room furnished more like a lady's boudoir than a man's dressing-room. A handsome dressing-table covered with a bewildering array of silver-topped bottles stands at the left. A large cheval glass stands in front of a bay window opening out on a balcony. The curtains are open. The door at the back leads into the* BEAU'S *bedroom. A table stands at one side with books and papers in precise order. A door at the left-hand side leads into an ante-room where visitors are detained until the great man wishes to see them.*

MORTIMER, *the* BEAU'S *valet and really confidential servant, is discovered sitting on sofa, head back, face covered with handkerchief; has evidently been asleep. It is about noon.*
  [MORTIMER *removes handkerchief, yawns and speaks.*]

MORTIMER.

Up till four this morning! It was pretty lively at the club last night, but I have lost all my beauty sleep to pay

[11]

BEAU BRUMMEL

for it. I don't know how much longer we will be able to continue this style of living. Our nerves will give out if our credit doesn't. Mr. Brummel only turned over twice and then took to his chocolate. That means he will only be half an hour at his bath—time for a nap.

[*Replaces handkerchief.*]
[*Enter* SIMPSON *through door from anteroom.* SIMPSON *is the regulation footman, with powdered hair and livery.*]

SIMPSON.
[*At Left.*] Mr. Mortimer, sir, Mr. Abrahams has just called. He particularly wishes to see you, sir.

[*Going toward* MORTIMER.]

MORTIMER.
[*Starting and removing handkerchief.*] Hang Abrahams, what's he after? Dear me! It can't be that he thinks of collecting those I. O. U.'s of mine. [*Rising.*]

SIMPSON.
[*Who has a great respect for* MORTIMER.]
[*Very deferentially.*] Been losing again, sir?

MORTIMER.
[*Loftily.*] Yes, Simpson, pretty high stakes last night, and one must play, you know.

SIMPSON.
Mr. Mortimer, sir, you couldn't propose me in your club, could you, sir?

MORTIMER.
[*Haughtily and then more kindly as he sees* SIMPSON'S *downcast face.*] No, Simpson, not in your present position, you know, but if you should ever raise yourself, depend upon me to use all my influence for you.

SIMPSON.
[*Gratefully.*] Oh, thank you, sir, I'm sure, [*going*] but what about Mr. Abrahams, sir?

[12]

BEAU BRUMMEL

MORTIMER.

[*Seating himself.*] Oh, damn Abrahams!

[*Enter* ABRAHAMS *from anteroom, hat and cane in hand.* ABRAHAMS *is the typical Jew money lender of the period, exaggerated in dress and manner.*]

ABRAHAMS.

[*As* ABRAHAMS *enters,* SIMPSON *crosses back of table and exits, giving* ABRAHAMS *a look of haughty disdain.*] No you don't, Mr. Mortimer; no, you don't, not yet. Where's your master?

MORTIMER.

Excuse me, where's my gentleman, you mean, Mr. Abrahams. [*Rising.*] I am a gentleman's gentleman; I have no master.

ABRAHAMS.

[*At left center.*] Oh, you haven't a master, haven't you? Well, now, suppose I was to come down on you with some of your little I. O. U.'s, I wonder then if you'd have a master. Where's Mr. Brummel?

MORTIMER.

Mr. Brummel has not yet appeared.

ABRAHAMS.

[*Sitting down as if to wait.*] Inform him that Mr. Abrahams wishes to see him.

MORTIMER.

[*Shocked.*] I repeat, sir, he is not up.

ABRAHAMS.

Well, then, my good fellow, it's time he were up. Tell him I said so.

MORTIMER.

It is as much as my position is worth, sir, to go to him at this hour. You must call again, Mr. Abrahams.

[13]

BEAU BRUMMEL

ABRAHAMS.

[*Rising.*] Call again! Call again! This is the seventh time I've called again.

MORTIMER.

[*Trying now to placate him.*] Yes—eh—if you please, Mr. Abrahams.

ABRAHAMS.

No, sir; I must see him now. I'm in need of money myself and I must get it from Mr. Brummel. My creditors are pressing me and they force me to do the same. [*Loudly.*] I regret the necessity, but I am determined upon seeing him.

MORTIMER.

[*Who is so shocked he can hardly speak.*] Not so loud, Mr. Abrahams, not so loud. If Mr. Brummel were to hear you, he'd be distressed. Besides, he never tolerates any one who raises his voice unnecessarily. If he should hear you, you might never be paid.

ABRAHAMS.

[*Aghast at the thought.*] What! [*Loudly.*]

MORTIMER

[*Hands raised in horror.*] Sh! Sh!

ABRAHAMS.

What! [*Whispering in* MORTIMER'S *ear.*]

MORTIMER.

[*Looking at* ABRAHAMS *out of the corner of his eye.*] Upon my honor, Mr. Brummel was saying only yesterday he thought he would pay Mr. Abrahams.

ABRAHAMS.

[*A little more calmly.*] Then why hasn't he done so?

MORTIMER.

Mr. Brummel only said it yesterday and Mr. Brummel never does anything in a hurry.

[14]

BEAU BRUMMEL

ABRAHAMS.

Is four years a hurry? Well, this is the last time that I
will be put off. Do you follow me—the last time. And now,
when am I to have your little sums?

MORTIMER.

[*Taking out handkerchief and wiping eyes.*] Mine! Oh,
I have a wealthy aunt, who is now dying in Clapham, Mr.
Abrahams, and I am her sole heir. I fear I must beg you
to wait until after her funeral.

ABRAHAMS.

[*At left center. Really puzzled.*] It is very strange, a very
large number of my clients have wealthy aunts who are
dying, but they don't die. They all appear to be affected
with a most lingering sickness. However, Mr. Brummel
has no such relative, and I believe, on consideration, that
I will wait for him this morning.   [*Sits in chair by table.*]

MORTIMER.

[*Who is now determined to get rid of him, crossing to*
ABRAHAMS.] No, really, Mr. Abrahams, you must go.
Mr. Brummel would not see you until his toilet is com-
pleted; and, indeed, if he would, he could transact no
business in *déshabille*.

ABRAHAMS.

In what? [*Jumps up.*] Oh, very well, very well; but
advise him this is the last time I will be dismissed without
seeing him. The next time I call I will see him whether he
is in desh—desh—or nothing. I will have my money. I
will have my money.

> [*All the while he is saying this* MORTIMER *is*
> *pushing him gently off through the anteroom.*
> MORTIMER *ushers* ABRAHAMS *off at the left,*
> *then crosses to the right center, and turns*
> *away with a sigh of relief as* SIMPSON *enters*
> *very hurriedly.*]

[15]

BEAU BRUMMEL

SIMPSON.

Mr. Mortimer, sir, there are a number of people waiting with their accounts to see Mr. Brummel. What shall I say, sir?

MORTIMER.

[*Resignedly.*] Get a list of their names, Simpson, and tell them I'll call around and see them to-day.

SIMPSON.

Very well, sir.

> [*Exit* SIMPSON *through anteroom. A murmur of voices is heard there.*]

MORTIMER.

Affairs are very shaky. It was only three days since Abrahams called. According to this he will return again to-morrow. [*Sits in chair in front of dressing-case, makes himself comfortable and is about to fall asleep when* KATHLEEN *appears at door and peeps in.*]

KATHLEEN.

> [*In door at left. Is Mariana's Irish maid, very pretty and piquant.*]

Pst! Pst!

> [MORTIMER *starts and listens, then composes himself for another nap.*]

KATHLEEN.

Pst! Pst!

MORTIMER.

[*Still seated.*] I did drink pretty heavily last night, but I hardly thought it affected me.

KATHLEEN.

Hello!

MORTIMER.

[*Rising.*] Who is it? What is it?

[16]

BEAU BRUMMEL

KATHLEEN.

[*Still in door. With pretty impatience.*] Is it all right, can I come in?

MORTIMER.

[*Laughingly.*] Look here, Kathleen, are you going to indulge in that sort of thing when we are married?

KATHLEEN.

Can I come in?   [*Comes in a few steps.*]

MORTIMER.

[*Crossing to center.*] Yes, it's all right now. Mr. Brummel is finishing the first part of his toilet; he won't be out for some time yet. Well, what do you want, you little minx?   [*Chucks her under chin.*]

KATHLEEN.

[*Tossing her head.*] Minx, indeed! [*Crossing to right.*] I dropped in to find out what's your intentions. Mr. Sheridan's gentleman has become very pressing, in his, and won't be held off much longer. Now, is it marriage with you, Mr. Mortimer, or is it a breaking off, Mr. Mortimer? Am I to be worn in your coat like a flower and thrown aside when I'm withered, or am I to be pressed in the album of your affections, Mr. Mortimer? I own there is an air about Mr. Brummel and I should not be averse to a connection with the family.   [*Quite seriously.*]

MORTIMER.

[*Just as seriously.*] And I mean you shall have it, Kathleen, for you would become our position. But the fact is, I can't afford to marry while Mr. Brummel's money matters are so bad. I tell you his social position is like a halo, it is glory all round him, but there's a hollow in the middle.

KATHLEEN.

[*With a sudden thought.*] Mr. Mortimer! We must marry Mr. Brummel! First, we must procure a list of the heiresses.

[17]

BEAU BRUMMEL

MORTIMER.

[*Slyly.*] I understand there is a heap of money in your family.

KATHLEEN.

[*Dubiously.*] But there's one obstacle—Miss Mariana's affections are already engaged.

MORTIMER.

Indeed, to whom?

KATHLEEN.

That's what I can't find out. The divvle never signs any of his letters. I can promise you one thing, he isn't very high, and Miss Mariana's father has forbid him the house and swears she shan't have him. Mr. Vincent, oh, ho! he's all for position and fashion.

MORTIMER.

[*Puts arm around her waist and they walk up and down.*] Then Mr. Vincent would be glad to marry her to Mr. Brummel. We'll enlist him on our side. Now there are two difficulties with Mr. Brummel—first, he is, just at present, very friendly with Mrs. St. Aubyn. Still I think I can get him out of that predicament, and then you see Mr. Brummel is so demmed particular, the young lady must be correct to a hair in every respect——

KATHLEEN.

[*Affectedly.*] Lord, Mr. Morty, you needn't worry yourself about that; ar'n't I in her service? And what's the matter with me? She's a very much *a la mud* and [*crosses to mirror at right*] correct in every particular. Mr. Mortimer, do you think you are as becoming to me as Mr. Sheridan's gentleman?

[*Beckoning to him, he comes up and looks over her shoulder in the glass.*]

MORTIMER.

[*Putting his arm around her and leading her away from*

[18]

BEAU BRUMMEL

mirror.] Look, here, Kathleen, no tricks; and what are you doing out at this time of day?

KATHLEEN.
[KATHLEEN *and* MORTIMER *walk to and fro.*] Why, Miss Mariana sent me over an hour back with this letter [*holding up letter*] for her young gentleman. They correspond through me; faith, I'm turned into a regular post-bag. But I'm afraid I've missed him this time.

MORTIMER.
[*Laughingly.*] You will have to miss him quite regularly when we begin to break it off between your young mistress and her lover and supplant him with my gentleman.

BEAU
[BEAU'S *voice in distance from bedroom.*]
Mortimer! Mortimer!

MORTIMER.
Yes, sir! [*Alarmed.*] That's Mr. Brummel!

KATHLEEN.
[*Starts off left.*] Lord! I'm off. [*Pointing to dressing table.*] Oh, Morty! Is that where he sits and does it? [MORTIMER *nods.*] Couldn't I see him?

MORTIMER.
[*With horror.*] What! Before he's finished? Gracious heavens! No!

KATHLEEN.
[*Crossing to door to anteroom.*] Well, I am going. I'm loathe to leave ye; good-by—be faithful. [*Throws kiss.*]

> [*Exit* KATHLEEN. *Enter* BEAU *from door into bedroom. He enters slowly as though it were too much trouble to come in. He is dressed in a yellow brocaded dressing-gown tied with a heavy yellow cord. It is long, so that*

[19]

BEAU BRUMMEL

only his patent leather pumps with silver buckles show, with just a glimpse of brown and yellow striped socks. He crosses at once to the dressing-table without paying any attention to MORTIMER, *who bows deferentially and says:*]

MORTIMER.
Good morning, sir.

BEAU.
Oh, go to the devil.

MORTIMER.
[*To himself.*] Mr. Brummel is in a bad temper this morning.

BEAU.
[*Seating himself at dressing-table.*] Mortimer, is the sun shining?

MORTIMER.
[*Crossing to window—right.*] Oh, finely, sir.
[SIMPSON *enters, bringing soda-water bottle and glass in a tray.*]

BEAU.
[*Simply looks at it and motions it away—exit* SIMPSON.]
Any gossip, Mortimer?
[*Has taken up hand-glass and then gently smooths his eyebrows.*]

MORTIMER.
None of any account, sir. The Dowager Lady Slopington ran off yesterday with young Philip Pettibone.

BEAU.
[BEAU *is now manicuring his nails.*]
If it happened yesterday, it must be forgotten to-day.

MORTIMER.
And Captain Badminton shot himself in the park last night, sir, after losing ten thousand pounds at hazard.

BEAU BRUMMEL

BEAU.

[*Now takes tweezers and pulls out one or two hairs from his face.*]

Very stupid of him; he should have shot himself first—is he dead, Mortimer?

MORTIMER.

No, sir.

BEAU.

He always was a bad shot. You'll find some of his I. O. U.'s among my papers; return them to him cancelled, with my compliments. He can use them for plasters. And who has called?

MORTIMER.

[*Crosses to small table and looks over cards.*] Oh, nobody, sir. To be sure there has been the usual crowd of people. The Hon. Mrs. Donner came for your subscription to the town charities, and I gave her all you could spare, sir. Mr. Cecil Serious, the poet, called for permission to inscribe your name under the dedication of his new volume of verses. Lord Cowden came to know if your influence might still be used in the support of his party in the coming elections.

BEAU.

[*Still occupied with his toilet.*] Yes, he can use my influence. Well, you satisfied them all, I presume.

MORTIMER.

[*At left.*] I took that liberty, sir. Then there was a quantity of trades people with their bills and accounts. I said you had been out all night with the Prince and really were not able to see them.

BEAU.

Pray, Mortimer, be a little careful of my reputation in your lies. You know common people are apt to look upon dissipation very differently from persons of fashion. You

BEAU BRUMMEL

may say what you like about the Prince, but handle me
a little delicately.

MORTIMER.

[*Bows, then speaks after short pause.*] Sprague, the
tailor, called again, sir, with his account.

BEAU.

[*Much astonished.*] Again! What insolence! Upon what
previous occasion had he the presumption to call?

MORTIMER.

A year ago last month, sir.

BEAU.

[*With real astonishment.*] What damned impudence!
Mortimer, you may let it be known at your club that he
comes to me no longer. Send for that new tailor—what's
his name—to wait upon me this afternoon. Bring this
morning's letters.

> [MORTIMER *brings down table with a number
> of little notes to* BEAU, *who is still seated at
> dressing-table.*]

MORTIMER.

[*Holding up a bundle of bills.*] These are bills, sir. All
of them fresh this morning and some of them more urgent
than usual.

BEAU.

[*Not taking the trouble to look at them.*] Hide them away
somewhere, where I can't see them, and I shall feel as if
they had been paid.

MORTIMER.

[*Pushing forward a bundle of notes.*] Your private correspondence, this little collection, sir.

BEAU.

[*Still seated, takes up notes one at a time and smells them.*]
Patchouli!—phew!—Frangipane!—I believe that smells

[22]

like peppermint. I don't know what that is, but it's very unpleasant. Violet!—musk! Take them all away—you may read them yourself.

MORTIMER.
[*Holding up yellow lock of hair which he has taken from an envelope.*] This letter has this little enclosure, sir.

BEAU.
[*In interested tone.*] Money?

MORTIMER.
Not exactly, sir, although a similar color.

BEAU.
[*Disappointed—languidly.*] Whose is it?

MORTIMER.
Lady Constance Conway's, and she says——

BEAU.
[*Interrupts him.*] Never mind what she says. I believe I did honor her with the request. Write and thank her and quote some poetry. Say hers is the most precious lock I possess. Rather tender little woman, Lady Constance.
[*Sentimentally.*]

MORTIMER.
[*Pointedly.*] Is she rich, sir?

BEAU.
[*Sighing.*] No, she's not.

MORTIMER.
[*Opening another note.*] Oh! A note from Mrs. St. Aubyn. She wants to know where you've been these two days. She says you are her lover's knot; she's coming to see you at three this afternoon, bids you be ready to receive her. She has, besides, down below in a postscript, a myriad of sentiments which she says belongs to you, and she is herself, unalterably yours, Horatia.

BEAU BRUMMEL

BEAU.

The one woman in London with whom it's possible to have a Platonic friendship. One must have something nowadays and these other liasons are so excessively vulgar.

MORTIMER.

[*Very loud as he opens letter.*] Mr. Brummel, sir.

BEAU.

[*Shocked.*] Mortimer, how often have I told you never to startle me?

MORTIMER.

[*Bows an apology.*] Mr. Brummel, sir, here's the memorandum of an I. O. U. for one thousand pounds, given by you to Lord Gainsby at White's three nights ago for sums lost at hazard.

BEAU.

[*A little disturbed.*] The deuce, Mortimer. It must be paid to-day; that's a debt of honor. How can we obtain the money?

MORTIMER.

I can try Abrahams again, sir, but he was very difficult the last time.

B——.

[*Rings bell. Enter* SIMPSON *from anteroom. Without looking at him.*] Simpson!

SIMPSON.

Yes, sir.

BEAU.

Go to Mr. Abrahams. Of course, you know where he lives.

SIMPSON.

Yes, sir.

[MORTIMER *brings table back to place up at right.*]

[24]

" Men shake hands much too often. A glance of the eye,
Reginald—a glance of the eye."

BEAU BRUMMEL

BEAU.

Say Mr. Brummel requests his immediate attendance.

SIMPSON.

Very well, sir!   [*Exit* SIMPSON.]

MORTIMER.

[*Coming down.*] Mr. Brummel, sir, this can't go on much longer.

BEAU.

No, I hope not.

MORTIMER.

Everybody's pressing on you and the only thing that keeps them off at all is your friendship with the Prince, and if anything should happen to that——

BEAU.

[*Quite unaffectedly.*] Nothing could happen to that, Mortimer, and if anything did, I should cut the Prince and make the old King the fashion.   [*Rises.*]

MORTIMER.

I have been wondering, Mr. Brummel, if I might be so bold, if you had ever thought, sir, of the advisability of a rich marriage.

BEAU.

Yes, it has occurred to me occasionally; in fact, it has passed through my mind quite recently that it might be desirable. Only to decide on the person really seems too difficult a task for me to undertake. You would not have me marry a mere money bag, would you, Mortimer?

MORTIMER.

[*At left of table.*] But the great Mr. Brummel has only to choose.

BEAU.

[*Staring at him in utter surprise that such a remark*

BEAU BRUMMEL

should be necessary.] Yes, of course! But one desires some sentiment. I wouldn't care to make a loan for life and give myself as security.

MORTIMER.

Mr. Brummel, sir, have you ever observed Miss Mariana Vincent?

BEAU.

[*Thoughtfully.*] Yes, I have noticed her in the Mall and I must confess it was to admire her; her person is perfect. Is her matrimonial figure as good?

MORTIMER.

I believe it is sixty thousand pounds, sir.

BEAU.

Oh, dear!

MORTIMER.

[*Hastily.*] But Mr. Vincent would be ashamed to offer so little to the wife of Mr. Brummel.

BEAU.

[*Musingly.*] Yes, it's a very paltry sum, and Mrs. St. Aubyn——

MORTIMER.

[*Insinuatingly.*] If you could present her to the Prince, Mr. Brummel, don't you think a Platonic friendship might spring up there?

BEAU.

[*As though thinking aloud.*] She is ambitious, but she is clever, and would never forgive a slight. She is a good hater and if she thought she were being put upon one side, she would make a sly enemy. Well—we shall see. Mortimer, write a letter to Mr. Vincent—make my proposal for his daughter's hand. Be mindful of your language and careful to accomplish it in the most elegant manner, and request an immediate reply.

[26]

BEAU BRUMMEL

MORTIMER.

Yes, sir.

SIMPSON.

[*Enters at left from anteroom.*] Mr. Reginald Courtenay, sir.

BEAU.

Yes, you may bid him come in here.

> [REGINALD *comes rushing in from anteroom.
> He is a handsome, bright-faced lad of twenty,
> dressed simply, in great contrast to* BEAU'S
> *gorgeous attire.*]

REGINALD.

[*Speaks very loud.*] Ah! Mortimer. [*Crossing to* BEAU, *after placing hat and cane on table, with hand extended.*] Good morning, Uncle Beau!

BEAU.

Reginald! You are evidently laboring under the impression that I am a great distance off.

> [MORTIMER *goes off into bedroom.*]

REGINALD.

[*In a much lower tone.*] I beg your pardon, Uncle Beau. [*Bows.*] Good morning. [*Hand extended.*]

BEAU.

No, I don't think I will shake hands; men shake hands much too often, especially in warm weather. A glance of the eye, Reginald—a glance of the eye. Did it ever occur to you, Reginald, how thoughtful our Creator was in giving us bodies, to give them to us naked, so that we could dress and ornament them as we choose?

REGINALD.

It had not occurred to me before, Uncle.

BEAU.

No, I suppose not.

[27]

BEAU BRUMMEL

REGINALD.

I trust you are well this morning?

BEAU.

No, I've contracted a cold—I suppose everybody will have a cold now. I left my carriage on the way to the Pavilion last night and the wretch of a landlord put me into the same room with a damp stranger.

REGINALD.

[*Goes up, sits on settee at right, with a change of tone and manner.*] Uncle, I want your advice and help.

BEAU.

[BEAU *goes to* REGINALD *and puts his hand on his shoulder and speaks with real affection.*] All the advice I have is yours. Reginald, my boy, I trust you haven't gotten yourself into difficulties. You are the one creature in the world whom I love, and I think it would break my heart to see you in any trouble from which I could not free you. Your mother, my boy, was a mother to me for years, and when I lost my sister, I lost the best friend I ever had. She saw the heart that beat beneath the waistcoat. More-over, she helped me always—in every way; if it had not been for her, perhaps even now, I might be in some smoky office in the city—that undiscovered country from whose bourn no social traveler ever returns. [*Crosses back to dressing-table.*] What is it, Reginald? If you are in debt I will give you a letter to Mr. Abrahams. If you are in the blue-devils I will give you one to Mrs. St. Aubyn.

REGINALD.

[*Rises and coming down to* BEAU.] I am in neither, Uncle Beau; I am in love.

BEAU.

Dear me, that's worse than either. How do you know you are?

[28]

BEAU BRUMMEL

REGINALD.

Why—well—I feel it here! [*Indicating heart.*] I live only when she is present and merely exist when away from her.

BEAU.

[*Staring at him through his glass.*] Reginald, don't talk like a family newspaper. Is your fair one possible?

REGINALD.

[*Indignantly.*] If you mean is she a gentlewoman, she is, and besides, young and beautiful—and——

BEAU.

[*At right.*] Of course, she would be. But does she return your passion?

REGINALD.

She loves me, Uncle.

BEAU.

Of course, she would—but——

REGINALD.

Her father is opposed to me. He has forbidden our seeing each other; our meetings have to be clandestine, and our mutual correspondence is carried on through her maid. He wishes a title for his daughter. He is rich and seeks only position in the world of society, while she, ah! she cares nothing for it—only—for—me.

BEAU.

[*Looking at him through glass.*] Reginald, do you know I think you are more conceited than I am.

REGINALD.

[*At center.*] Oh, no! [*Bowing.*] Oh! Uncle Beau, you, who are so high in favor at the Court, who have Dukes at your elbow and the Regent on your arm, might help me in a worldly way that I might win over the father. I know that I am dear to you, as you are to me—and that is why I have come to you.

[29]

BEAU BRUMMEL

BEAU.

And you shall not have come in vain. [*With enthusiasm.*] By my manners! You shall have the girl if I have to plead for you myself. But that will not be necessary. No, I will give you social distinction and prominence much more easily. Come for me in a little while and I'll walk along the Mall with you to White's. Yes, and be seen with you at the club window a few moments. Now, my dear boy, can anybody possibly do anything more for you?
[*With absolute conviction.*]

REGINALD.

[*Pleased.*] No, Uncle. [*Turning to go.*] Yes, Uncle— you can do one thing more for me. I've left my purse; will you lend me a couple of crowns to take a chair with? I've missed an appointment with the maid, and I wish to return to the park in a hurry.

BEAU.

Reginald, you know I never use silver, it's so excessively dirty and heavy. Ask Mortimer for a couple of guineas as you go out. [REGINALD *starts to go.*] By the way, Reginald, it is just possible that I may enter into the golden bands myself. I am thinking somewhat of a marriage with a certain young lady whose charms, strange to say, very much resemble those you would have described had I permitted you to inflict me.

REGINALD.

[*Laughing.*] You marry! Uncle! You! Your wit makes me laugh in spite of my dolours. Imagine the great Beau Brummel married! Why, Uncle, your children would be little Rosettes.

BEAU.

[*Wincing.*] Reginald, never be guilty of a pun; it is excessively vulgar. I am serious. I think I may marry.

[30]

BEAU BRUMMEL

REGINALD.
[*Going to* BEAU *and offering hand quickly.*] Then, Uncle, I am glad for you.

BEAU.
[*Starts, looks at hand with eye-glass.*] Dear me, what's that? Oh, dear, no, Reginald—a glance of the eye. [REGINALD *drops hand.*] A glance of the eye. My boy, you look so like your mother—God bless you.

[REGINALD *goes to table at left for hat and stick.*]

BEAU.
You will return?

REGINALD.
[*Boisterously, crossing to door at left.*] Yes, shortly.

BEAU.
[*Again shocked at his loud tone.*] Reginald!

[REGINALD *stops, returns a step or two, looks at* BEAU *as if to say, "What is it?"* BEAU *bows very politely.* REGINALD *remembers he'd forgotten himself for a minute, bows, places hat on his head, as he turns, and exits less boisterously.*]

SIMPSON.
[*Enters from anteroom as* REGINALD *exits.*] Mr. Abrahams, sir.

BEAU.
Yes, you can let him in here.

SIMPSON.
[*Exits and returns, ushering in* ABRAHAMS.] Mr. Abrahams, sir.

ABRAHAMS.
[*Enters with assurance.*] I understand, Mr. Brummel, that you wished to see me. I had much difficulty in leaving my place of business, but you see I am here.

[31]

BEAU BRUMMEL

BEAU.

[*Glancing at him through his glass.*] Ah—Abrahams—
ah, yes! So you are, so you are.

ABRAHAMS.

[*Insinuatingly.*] I thought it was likely, sir, that you
wished to make a few payments.

BEAU.

[*Drily.*] I think that's wrong, Abrahams; do you know
I fear you will have to guess again.

ABRAHAMS.

[*With indignation.*] Well now, really, Mr. Brummel,
I hope you don't want to raise another loan.

BEAU.

[*Pleased that he has surmised it.*] I believe that's right,
Abrahams; second thoughts seem to be always the best.

ABRAHAMS.

[*Very loudly.*] Really, Mr. Brummel, sir, I'm sorry,
sir, but the fact is I can't possibly——

[*Enter Simpson from anteroom.*]

SIMPSON.

[*Interrupting* ABRAHAMS.] A footman from His Royal
Highness, the Prince Regent, sir.

BEAU.

[*Quite unconcernedly.*] Yes, you can let him come in
here.

[ABRAHAMS *looks at* BEAU *and backs up a trifle.*
Enter footman. Stands below door.]

BEAU.

[*Without looking at him.*] Mortimer, which one is it?

MORTIMER.

[*Who had come in from bedroom.*] Bendon, sir.

[32]

BEAU BRUMMEL

BEAU.

[*At right. Graciously.*] Very well, Bendon.

FOOTMAN.

[*With great respect.*] Mr. Brummel, sir, His Royal Highness wishes to know if you will be at home this afternoon at four o'clock. If so, he will call upon you to make arrangements for the dance at Carlton House.

BEAU.

At what o'clock did you say, Bendon?

BENDON.

[*With low bow.*] At four o'clock, sir.

BEAU.

Say to His Royal Highness to make it half-past four o'clock.

> [*Exit footman at left, followed by* SIMPSON. ABRAHAMS *is overcome with wonder at this and looks at* MORTIMER, *who draws himself up proudly.*]

BEAU.

[*As if recollecting his presence.*] You were saying, Mr. Abrahams, that you could not possibly——

ABRAHAMS.

[*Bowing, changing attitude and tone.*] Hm, ach—hem— that I should be very glad—though I am just now rather pressed myself. How much did you say, sir?

BEAU.

How much did I say, Mortimer?

> [*Enter* REGINALD *same door.*]

REGINALD.

[*Boisteriously rushing to* BEAU, *left center.*] Am I in good time, Uncle?

[33]

BEAU.

[*Startled.*] Reginald, how often have I told you to
enter a room properly. You came in like—like a——
Mortimer, what did Mr. Reginald come like?

MORTIMER.

[*Reproachfully.*] Like a thunderbolt, sir.

BEAU.

Ah, yes—like a thunderbolt; very unpleasant things,
thunderbolts. Mortimer, have I ever seen a thunderbolt?

MORTIMER

Once, sir.

BEAU.

Yes; I once saw a thunderbolt; very unpleasant things,
thunderbolts. You must not come in like a thunderbolt,
Reginald.

REGINALD.

[*Looking at* ABRAHAMS.] I beg your pardon, Uncle
Beau. Are you busy?

BEAU.

[*As if startled.*] I beg your pardon——

REGINALD.

Are you busy?

BEAU.

Busy! Ugh! Never employ that term with me. No
gentleman is ever busy. Insects and city people are busy.
This—ah—person has come to ask my assistance in some
little financial matters, and I think I've rather promised
to oblige him. Mortimer, go with this—ah—ah—person.
You go with my valet. [ABRAHAMS *bows and bows.*] Yes,
quite so, quite so.

> [*Exit* MORTIMER *and* ABRAHAMS *into ante-
> room at left,* ABRAHAMS *backing, bowing all
> the time.*]

BEAU BRUMMEL

REGINALD.

[*Gloomily sitting on sofa.*] I was too late; I missed her.

BEAU.

Don't be gloomy, Reginald, or I shall not be able to walk with you. Nothing is more conspicuous than melancholy.

[MORTIMER *returns—coughs.*]

BEAU.

Mortimer, are you coughing?

MORTIMER.

[*Apologetically.*] Yes, sir.

BEAU.

[*At right.*] Well, I wish you wouldn't. You wish to speak with me?

MORTIMER.

Yes, sir. [BEAU *crosses, bowing in apology as he passes* REGINALD.] Mr. Brummel, sir, everything is arranged satisfactorily, sir.

BEAU.

Did you send for the new tailor, what's his name, to come this afternoon?

MORTIMER.

Yes, sir.

BEAU.

And have you written the letter to Mr. Vincent?

MORTIMER.

Yes, sir, all ready to seal.

BEAU.

Then seal it and despatch it at once. And now, Reginald, come with me and you shall see me having my coat put on. [REGINALD *rises.*]

[35]

BEAU BRUMMEL

[*Exit* BEAU *and* REGINALD *into bedroom. Enter* KATHLEEN *from anteroom.*]

KATHLEEN.

La! I must come in for a minute. I missed my young gentleman in the park and I ventured back to ask how we are to discover who he is. That's what we must do somehow, but how?

[REGINALD *enters from bedroom.*]

REGINALD.

[*Coming down.*] Mr. Brummel's snuff-box, Mortimer.

[REGINALD *and* KATHLEEN *recognize each other.*]

REGINALD.

Her maid!

KATHLEEN.

[*To* MORTIMER.] Oh, Lord! The very young gentleman himself.

MORTIMER.

What!

REGINALD.

[*At left. Suspiciously.*] What are you doing here?

KATHLEEN.

[*At center.*] Why, I missed you in the park, sir—you were too early. [*To* MORTIMER.] Will you say something? But I saw you in advance of me. [*To* MORTIMER.] Give utterance to something. And I followed you here to give you this letter. [*Gives note to* REGINALD. *To* MORTIMER.] I had to give it to him that time.

BEAU.

[*Outside calling.*] Reginald!

[MORTIMER *and* REGINALD *rush* KATHLEEN *off through bay window.* MORTIMER *stands at window after drawing curtain.* REGINALD

[36]

crosses to table at left center, stands back of same. Enter BEAU *from bedroom.*]

BEAU.

[*At center door.*] Mortimer, what was that extraordinary commotion?

MORTIMER.

[*At right at window, innocently.*] What commotion, sir?

BEAU.

[*Standing in doorway.*] Mortimer, don't be an echo; how often have I told you that servants are born to answer questions, not to ask them? I believe you said the sun was shining? [*Crosses to window.*]

REGINALD.

[*Very loud, stopping him.*] Uncle Beau, your snuff-box.
[*Offering box.*]

BEAU.

[*At center. Starts.*] Ah! I knew I lacked something; I perceived I had on my coat, my fob, my waistcoat, my unmentionables. Dear me, yes, it was my snuff-box— thank you, thank you. [*He does not take snuff-box.*]

> [*He now is fully dressed—long brown trousers, fitting very closely around the leg and buttoned around the ankle, a yellow brocaded waistcoat, brown coat, ruffled shirt with neckerchief, fob with many seals. He crosses to dressing-table and arranges flowers—three yellow roses—in his coat.* MORTIMER *has crossed to table and stands holding hat, gloves and stick.* REGINALD *has the snuff-box.* BEAU *turns from dressing-table, comes to the center.* REGINALD *offers him the snuff-box open.* BEAU *takes pinch with courteous nod of head.* REGINALD *takes pinch, closes*

BEAU BRUMMEL

box, hands it to BEAU, *who holds it in hand.* MORTIMER
then hands him gloves. BEAU *arranges
them in hand very precisely.* MORTIMER
then hands stick. BEAU *puts this in just
right position.* MORTIMER *then hands hat.*
BEAU *takes it, is about to put it on, then
looks at it, stands aghast and hands it back
with no word, but just an expression of
complete astonishment.* MORTIMER, *very
puzzled, takes it and then sees that he has
handed it with the wrong side to put on.
Bows very low with an expression of great
chagrin. Turns it and hands it to* BEAU.
BEAU *takes it, walks to mirror, raises it two
or three times until he has it at just the right
angle, then puts it on. Turns to* REGINALD.]

BEAU.

And now, REGINALD, I'll make your fortune for you.
I'll walk down the Mall with you to White's.

[*Walks to door followed by* REGINALD *as curtain comes down.*]

THE FIRST ACT

SCENE TWO

BEAU BRUMMEL

THE FIRST ACT

SCENE TWO

The BEAU'S *reception-room. A small room, furnished in chintz. Chippendale sofa at the right. Large entrance at back with red striped chintz curtains. Palms in window. A table on the left holds a standing memorandum tablet. Small arm-chair back of sofa. Two or three other chairs scattered around the room. A door at the left.* BEAU BRUMMEL *at the rise of curtain is standing by table, looking at the memorandum tablet through his eye-glass. He is dressed as in scene one.* SIMPSON *draws the curtains at the back, and announces:*

SIMPSON.

Mrs. St. Aubyn, sir!
>[SIMPSON *then leaves the curtains drawn and goes out.* BEAU *turns and bows.*]

BEAU.

Punctual as the day and twice as welcome.
>[MRS. ST. AUBYN *has sailed into the room with an air that plainly says, "You and I are to settle some important things to-day." She is a very handsome woman of about thirty, beautifully dressed, and showing in every look and motion the woman accustomed to homage and command. She carries a fan, which she uses to emphasize all her remarks.*]

MRS. ST. AUBYN.

You received my letter?

BEAU.

[*With another bow.*] And your ambrosial lock of hair.
>[MRS. ST. AUBYN *is at first offended, and then laughs and sits on sofa.*]

[41]

BEAU BRUMMEL

MRS. ST. AUBYN.

Not mine, my dear BEAU; you know I'm not such a fool.

[BEAU *is not at all taken aback by the mistake he has made.*]

BEAU.

Ah, no, I believe I am mistaken; but, my dear Horatia, one gets things of this sort so mixed; and I plead in extenuation that the wish was father to the thought.

[BEAU *sits in chair near table.*]

MRS. ST. AUBYN.

Have you missed me really these last two days? Where have you been? It's been so dull without you, I vow, I could almost have married again. [*Leans forward and speaks very confidentially.*] Now, I want you to do me a favor, will you?

BEAU.

Whisper it and it is done.

MRS. ST. AUBYN.

Well, then, I will whisper. I want you to get me a card to the dance at Carlton House.

BEAU.

The very privilege that I have looked forward to. I desire to present you myself to the Prince, and witness your triumph. An unselfish pleasure, you would say, but I love you too well, my dear Horatia, not to sacrifice myself to your greatest opportunity.

[*During this speech* MRS. ST. AUBYN *has listened with a slight cynical smile, and now with an air of finality says* :]

MRS. ST. AUBYN.

I would not give up your devotion altogether—even for the Prince's.   [*With great empressement.*]

[42]

BEAU BRUMMEL

BEAU.

Take both.   Mine you will always have.

MRS. ST. AUBYN.

Yet I think my devotion for you overbalances yours.

BEAU.

My dear madam, you are too good.   Do you know, I fear you will die young?

MRS. ST. AUBYN.

[*With an air of giving up this contest of wits.*]   Oh, the deuce take your fine phrases!   If I thought I'd a rival, I'd let the Prince flit somewhere else.   You're clever, and the Prince isn't.   He'll be very dull.   Then he'll be harder to keep within bounds.   Oh, [*quickly as she sees an almost imperceptible shrug of* BEAU's *shoulder*] it isn't that I'm afraid for my reputation, that was damned long ago.   But I've certain notions of self-respect which aren't in the fashion and which men don't seem to understand.

BEAU.

[*Very quietly.*]   Marry him!

MRS. ST. AUBYN.

[*With real astonishment.*]   What!

BEAU.

[*Taking out snuff-box and taking snuff.*]   Marry him.

MRS. ST. AUBYN.

It is impossible!

BEAU.

With you all things are possible.

> [MRS. ST. AUBYN *laughs nervously and steals a surreptitious look at herself in a little mirror in her fan.*]

MRS. ST. AUBYN.

My dear Beau, I wish you'd make plain sense instead

[43]

BEAU BRUMMEL

of pretty sentences. What advantages have I to recommend me?

BEAU.

I will ask Mortimer to make out a list, but I may name one only—which is all sufficient. For the past six weeks —I have admired you.

[MRS. ST. AUBYN *rises with a laugh.*]

MRS. ST. AUBYN.

Oh, the conceit of the man. But tell me what style of woman is the Prince caught by?

[BEAU *rising also.*]

BEAU.

To be perfectly frank with you, the Prince admires the fashion and I—have made you the fashion. I am expecting him here this afternoon.

[MRS. ST. AUBYN *gives a shriek of dismay.*]

MRS. ST. AUBYN.

Who? The Prince! Gracious, why didn't you tell me? [*Runs to cheval glass.*] How am I looking? There, there, you needn't answer; I know it is one of my bad days.

[BEAU *is really very much upset by this rushing around and rapid talking. Speaks as though quite overcome.*]

BEAU.

My dear Horatia, I beg of you not to rattle on so; you've no idea how you fatigue me.

[SIMPSON *enters at back and announces:*]

SIMPSON.

The Duchess of Leamington, Mr. Sheridan, sir!

[SIMPSON *goes out.*]
[MRS. ST. AUBYN *says to herself, as she comes down to chair at right of sofa:*]

[44]

BEAU BRUMMEL

MRS. ST. AUBYN.

Damme that woman.

> [*The* DUCHESS *and* MR. SHERIDAN *enter at back. The* DUCHESS *is a very much painted and bewigged old young woman, dressed in a very light flowered gown, with a very large hat.* SHERIDAN *is still handsome, but no longer young, dressed in black silk knee breeches, black coat and stockings, wears the powdered wig instead of short hair like* BEAU'S. *The* DUCHESS *makes low curtsy to* BEAU, *who bows.*]

BEAU.

Ah, Duchess, what happy accident! Has your carriage broken down at my door, or do you come out of your own sweet charity? We were just speaking of you. I said you were the best-dressed woman in London, but Mrs. St. Aubyn did not seem to agree with me. [*To* SHERIDAN.] How do you do, Sherry?

> [*Nods to* SHERRY *and crossing to him, offers him snuff-box.* SHERIDAN *takes snuff.*]

DUCHESS.

[*The* DUCHESS, *as though noticing* MRS. ST. AUBYN *for the first time, says superciliously*:] How dy'e do?

MRS. ST. AUBYN.

[*Haughtily.*] Mr. Brummel pleases to be witty at my expense, Duchess. [*Then to herself.*] I must be on my guard. I don't understand Beau.

> [*The* DUCHESS *seats herself on sofa.* MRS. ST. AUBYN *is sitting in chair just below sofa.* BEAU *is sitting at chair near table and* SHERIDAN *is still standing.*]

DUCHESS.

Mr. Sheridan and I thought we'd come to tell you the

[45]

BEAU BRUMMEL

news. We knew you were never up till noon and thought you might want to hear what's going on.

> [SHERIDAN *now brings down chair from the back and sits about center.*]

SHERIDAN.

And when we were nearly here we remembered that really there was nothing to tell. There seems to be a lamentable dearth of scandal and gossip nowadays. I don't know what we are coming to. The ladies have absolutely nothing to talk about.

BEAU.

Sherry, I hear the "School for Scandal" is to be revived. It returns to us every year like spring and the influenza.

SHERIDAN.

[*Regretfully.*] Yes, but it won't be played as it used to be.

BEAU.

[*Thankfully.*] No, I hope not.

DUCHESS.

Dear me, only think of Miss Motional playing *Lady Teazle* now, at her age. Why is it that passé people are always so anxious to act? [*With a little affected giggle.*] I wonder you don't go on the stage, Mrs. St. Aubyn?

MRS. ST. AUBYN.

[*With great sweetness.*] I never experienced a scandal of sufficient *éclat* to warrant such a step. But, you, Duchess, what a success you would have!

DUCHESS.

Spiteful creature.

BEAU.

How very severe——

> [SIMPSON *enters at back, announces:*]

[46]

BEAU BRUMMEL

SIMPSON.

His Royal Highness, the Prince Regent, sir.

[SIMPSON *exits. The* PRINCE *enters, does not remove his hat. All rise.* DUCHESS *and* MRS. ST. AUBYN *curtsy.* SHERIDAN *bows very low and* BEAU *bows rather condescendingly.*]

PRINCE.

Ah, Beau, good morning.

BEAU.

This is very good of you, sir. The Duchess, I am sure, is a welcome vision. Sherry, you know, and you have heard—surely you have heard of the fascinating Mrs. St. Aubyn.

PRINCE.

But never have seen half enough.

BEAU.

Where will you put yourself, sir?

PRINCE.

[*Very emphatically says as he crosses to sofa:*] Damme, here.

[*He sits on sofa and makes a motion with his hand, inviting* MRS. ST. AUBYN *to sit beside him. To do this* MRS. ST. AUBYN *has to cross in front of the* DUCHESS, *which she does with a look of triumph, while the* DUCHESS *in moving to* MRS. ST. AUBYN'S *vacated seat turns up her nose as much as to say, "That won't last long." And* BEAU, *having witnessed all this little byplay, has a little smile as he sees all is just as he wants it.*]

MRS. ST. AUBYN.

I believe, sir, Mr. Sheridan is thinking of a new play.

[47]

BEAU BRUMMEL

PRINCE.

Don't you put me in, Sherry, or, if you do, mind you make me thin. A fat man played me in the pantomime t'other night, and damme, I had him locked up.

SHERIDAN.

[*With great deference.*] 'Twas a libel, sir, a gross libel.

PRINCE.

I heard, Beau, from my tailor this morning that you had gotten up something new in trousers. Why the deuce haven't you told me?

DUCHESS

[*With affected girlishness.*] Oh, dear me, what are the new trousers?

SHERIDAN

[*Maliciously.*] Why, Duchess, I don't see how they can possibly interest you.

MRS. ST. AUBYN.

Mr. Sheridan, Mr. Sheridan, both your plays and your conversation ought to be expurgated.

DUCHESS.

Come, come, stop all this banter, and Mr. Brummel will tell us.

BEAU.

[*As though bored by all this chatter.*] You must excuse me, Duchess; I have contracted a cold.

PRINCE.

I'll tell you, Duchess; they're long trousers which are slit so [*pointing with his cane to his own leg*] at the bottom and then buttoned tight. Very odd, you see, and striking.

DUCHESS.

It might be too striking; don't you think it depends on the—eh—eh—circumstances?

[48]

BEAU BRUMMEL

[*She draws her skirt up very slightly and strikes her leg with her fan.*]

P R I N C E.
Damme, Duchess, you're right; and that's just what I want to know of Beau here, whether he thinks my legs could stand 'em.

B E A U.
Really, my dear fellow, I'm no judge of calves.
[*All laugh.*]

S H E R I D A N.
You must appeal to the ladies, sir.

M R S. S T. A U B Y N.
[*Feigning to hide face with her fan.*] No, no; I object.

B E A U.
Mrs. St. Aubyn means they are little trifles not worth mentioning.

P R I N C E.
Now, I object. Besides, I've something else to talk about. What think you, Beau, of Tuesday week for the dance at Carlton House?
[BEAU *rises very slowly, takes tablet, looks it over*]

B E A U.
Tuesday, Tuesday, yes, I think I might make Tuesday do.
[PRINCE *rises, and everybody rises.*]

P R I N C E.
[*To* MRS. ST. AUBYN.] You will not forget, then, siren, the opening quadrille with me. May I take you to your chair?
[MRS. ST. AUBYN *makes him a low curtsy.*]

[49]

BEAU BRUMMEL

MRS. ST. AUBYN.

You make me wish my chair was at my own door instead of at Mr. Brummel's.

BEAU.

That's very good, very good.

> [MRS. ST. AUBYN *curtsies with a look of triumph to the* DUCHESS. *The* PRINCE *holds out his hand. She places her hand lightly on his, curtsies low to* BEAU, *and retires up to the center door, while the* PRINCE *is making his adieus, which he does by simply nodding to the* DUCHESS *and* SHERIDAN, *most graciously nodding to* BEAU, *and then takes* MRS. ST. AUBYN'S *hand again and they go off chattering.*]

DUCHESS.

[*Who has witnessed this with ill-concealed envy.*] Now, Mr. Brummel, promise me you'll bow to me at the play to-night. You bowed to Lady Farthingale last week Thursday, and she has given herself airs ever since.

BEAU.

After the play, Duchess, after the play. If I looked at you once during the play, I could never bend my attention again to the players.

DUCHESS.

[*With a girlish giggle.*] And that, Mr. Brummel, would damn the play.

BEAU.

Yes, I shouldn't wonder if it did. It wouldn't be the first play I've damned. [DUCHESS *curtsies,* SHERIDAN *bows, and they go off at center door.* BEAU *takes up memorandum tablet and goes toward door, left, reading as he*

BEAU BRUMMEL

goes.] Let me see, Thursday, lunch with Lord and **Lady** Pleasant, then on to Mrs. Hearsays—*pour passer le temps.* Dinner with the Dowager Countess of Alimony, dance at Gordon House, then to the Rag, then to the Raleigh, then to Vauxhall. [BEAU *goes out.*]

[SIMPSON *enters at center door, showing in* MR. VINCENT. VINCENT *is a stout, red-faced man, bluff manner, dressed rather loudly, brown bob-wig, drops his h's.*]

SIMPSON.

Whom shall I say, sir?

VINCENT.

Never mind introducing me. I'll introduce myself— tell him a gentleman wishes to see him in answer to his message; he'll understand.

SIMPSON.

Yes, sir.

[*Simpson goes out at left door with a look of disdain at* VINCENT.]

VINCENT.

[*Who is in a state of great excitement.*] Well, am I really in the great Mr. Brummel's house? I thought I'd show my appreciation of the honor I feel in Mr. Brummel's suit for my daughter's 'and by answering his message in person. But, really, now I'm 'ere, I'm not sure I've done the right thing. It's perfectly absurd, ridiculous, but I'm slightly nervous. I, the most successful cloth merchant of the day— unreasonable! I must appear at my ease or I shall fail to make an impression. Let me see, what shall I say when he comes in? After greeting him cordially, but with dignity, which is due to my position, I'll tell him in the proper language, with a few figures of speech to show I'm a man of some learning—he's coming.

[51]

BEAU BRUMMEL

[*Shows great nervousness. Begins to bow very low, moving first on one foot, then on the other, rubbing his hands together.*]

BEAU.

[*Enters from left door, tablet in hand, as he comes on says*:] Sunday—Sunday!——

VINCENT.

He's coming, he's coming!

BEAU.

Sunday after service, lunch with Lady Sybilla—Sybilla! She is "*un tant soit peu passé*," but there was a time, there was a time, when poor Sybilla and I——

[VINCENT'S *bowings and movements now attract* BEAU'S *attention, and he looks at him through eye-glass.*]

BEAU.

[*To himself.*] Ah, yes, the new tailor. [*Aloud.*] I will speak with you presently. I am somewhat occupied just now. [*Resumes soliloquy.*] Dinner with Figgles—silly beast, Figgles, but delicious truffles.

[VINCENT *has still continued to bow.*]

BEAU.

[*Looks at him again.*] Would you be so kind as not to wobble about in that way?

[VINCENT *stops a moment.*]

BEAU.

Thank you. [*Resumes soliloquy.*] Then on to Lady Ancient's—very tedious, but I must go or the poor woman's rooms would be quite vacant.

[VINCENT *has again resumed his bowing and clasping and unclasping his hands.*]

BEAU.

[*Looks at him.*] Did you hear what I observed? Would you be kind enough not to wobble about in that way, and

[52]

please do not wash your hands incessantly with imaginary soap, or chassez about in that manner? You have no idea how you distress me. [VINCENT *never stops, growing more and more nervous*.] How very extraordinary; he does not seem to be able to stop. Perhaps he is suffering with St. Vitus's dance. I shall never be able to employ a person so afflicted. Well, I won't dismiss him at once. I'll turn my back on him so I can't see him. [BEAU *turns his back to* VINCENT.] Let me see, where was I—ah—yes, Lady Ancient's very tedious, but I must go or the poor woman's rooms will be quite empty, then on to the club.

VINCENT.

[*Very deprecatingly*.] But, sir——

BEAU.

I'll speak with you presently. I am somewhat occupied just now, and, although my back is turned, I can feel you are wobbling about. [*To himself*.] I think I might venture to play again with my present prospects, Monday —Monday——

VINCENT.

[*Who is now getting restive and realizes he is being treated badly*.] But l——

BEAU.

Please do not say "but" again.

VINCENT.

My lord!——

BEAU.

Nothing so commonplace.

VINCENT.

Sir——

BEAU.

Very well, I suppose I had better speak with him—the sooner it is over the better. You've come to see me about my suit, I suppose.

BEAU BRUMMEL

VINCENT.

Yes, the honor it confers upon my daughter and my-self——

BEAU.

It's affected his head. Does your daughter sew, also?

VINCENT.

[*Surprised.*] Oh, beautifully, Mr. Brummel, but——

BEAU.

I must ask you to omit your "buts." Now if you will stand perfectly still for a few moments, I will endeavor to ask you one or two questions, but you must try to stand still, and if you try very hard you may succeed. But do try—there's a good man—try, try, try again. [*Aside.*] I'm so sorry for him. He must suffer so. Well, I won't look at him. [*Turns away and sits down at table. During all this time* VINCENT *has been bowing, trying to stand still, but not succeeding, owing to his great embarrassment.*] Now, have you any new cloths?

VINCENT.

My dear sir, I was not aware that you were at all interested in cloths.

[*Looks around for a chair and goes up to back of room to get one.*]

BEAU.

He's violent—he's going to attack me.

VINCENT.

[*Bringing down the chair near to* BEAU.] Yes, there are some very fine new cloths. Now, if you'll allow me——

BEAU.

Certainly not, sir; certainly not. [*Aside.*] Poor man, I suppose he never waited upon any one before.

VINCENT.

[*Can now stand it no longer, rises.*] This is too much.

[54]

'Tis outrageous. I'll not stand it, sir. I am a gentleman, sir.

BEAU.

Then why don't you behave like one?

VINCENT.

I've come here——

BEAU.

Of course, you've come here, that's very evident. You've come in answer to my message, haven't you?

VINCENT.

Yes, sir, I've come in answer to your message asking for my daughter's 'and——

BEAU.

Your daughter's what?

VINCENT.

My daughter's 'and——

BEAU.

Your daughter's hand? [*It begins to dawn upon him.*] I beg your pardon.

VINCENT.

I came to accept your offer of marriage, but I've altered my intention.

BEAU.

Dear me, you are——

VINCENT.

Mr. Holiver Vincent, sir.

BEAU.

[*Aside.*] And I thought he was the tailor. [*Aloud.*] A thousand apologies; won't you be seated? I was very much preoccupied. I ask you a thousand pardons—but [VINCENT *has begun to bow and wobble again*] what can you

expect if you will wobble about in that manner, my dear *Sir* Oliver!

[VINCENT, *indignant, again is soothed by title.*]

VINCENT.
Not *Sir* Holiver yet. *Mr.* Holiver—Mr. Holiver Vincent, at your service.

BEAU.
I only regret that you did not say so before.

[SIMPSON *enters at antedoor.*]

SIMPSON.
Sir, the Duke of York sends word will you be so gracious as to take mutton with him to-night?

[BEAU *looks at* VINCENT, *who looks pleadingly at him as much as to say, "Dine with me."*]

BEAU.
Send my polite regrets to his Royal Highness and say, I dine to-night with Mr. Oliver Vincent.

[SIMPSON *exits at center door.* BEAU *offers his snuff-box to Vincent, who takes a pinch and snuffs it with a loud, disagreeable noise, which shocks* BEAU *unspeakably.*]

THE CURTAIN FALLS ON THIS

THE SECOND ACT

THE SECOND ACT

The ballroom at Carlton House, a large, stately room hung in yellow damask—yellow damask furniture. On the right, a door leading into reception room. On the left are three curtained recesses. At the back a large doorway extends the whole width of room; it is curtained with yellow brocade curtains, which are looped back, showing a long hall hung with mirrors; it leads to supper room.

On the stage, at rise of curtain, are the PRINCE, *standing near the center talking to* MRS. ST. AUBYN. *The* PRINCE *is dressed in black, with the blue ribbon of the Garter;* MRS. ST. AUBYN *in elaborate evening dress.* SHERIDAN, *the* DUCHESS OF LEAMINGTON, LADY FARTHINGALE, LORD MANLY *and other guests are standing at back.*

PRINCE.

[*A little impatiently, as though he had been welcoming guests until tired.*] Any one else, damme; I'm ready to dance.   [*Servant enters from the door on the right.*]

SERVANT.

Mr. Brummel, Mr. Oliver Vincent, Miss Vincent.
    [SERVANT *steps to one side of door as* MR. BRUMMEL *comes in with* MARIANA, *her hand*

BEAU BRUMMEL

resting lightly on his. The DUCHESS *then steps forward and takes* MARIANA'S *hand.* MR. BRUMMEL *steps back to the side of* VINCENT, *who has followed them on. The* DUCHESS *leads* MARIANA *to the* PRINCE. *While this is going on* MRS. ST. AUBYN, *who has stared in amazement, says* :]

MRS. ST. AUBYN.
What's this presentation for; does it mean money for the Duchess? She does not need it.

DUCHESS.
[*As she presents* MARIANA.] Your Royal Highness— Miss Vincent.   [*Both curtsy to the* PRINCE.]

PRINCE.
This places me deeper than ever in Mr. Brummel's debt.
[*The* DUCHESS *and* MARIANA *back away and retire to the back of room, where they are joined by* SHERIDAN. BEAU *now advances to the* PRINCE, *closely followed by* VINCENT, *who is greatly excited.*]

BEAU.
Sir, I have the honor to present my friend, Mr. Oliver Vincent.

MRS. ST. AUBYN.
[*Aside.*] It's Mr. Brummel who is at the bottom of this. I think I begin to see.

PRINCE.
Mr. Vincent? Is this *the* Mr. Vincent, of the city? For, Egad, sir, I am pleased——

VINCENT.
[*Greatly embarrassed.*] Your Highness, sir, the honor is all mine, ah, all mine, Your Highness, thank you for your cordiality, Your Highness.

[60]

BEAU BRUMMEL

[*Offers the* PRINCE *his hand.* BEAU *quietly throws it up
and motions* VINCENT *away to the back,
covering his retreat, as it were, by his own
self-possession and the look of humorous
appeal which he gives to the* PRINCE.]

MRS. ST. AUBYN.

Your Royal Highness, what does Beau mean? Really,
sir, I think you take too much from him. They are from
the city, these Vincents; you can see its dust on their feet.

PRINCE.

[*Chuckling at his own wit.*] Yes, damme, madam; but
it's gold dust.

MRS. ST. AUBYN.

[*With a slight smile, such as an offended goddess might
give.*] Pray, sir, let us have the dance now.

[*The* PRINCE *offers her his hand and they take
their places at the head of set.* SHERIDAN
leads the DUCHESS *to one side.* LORD MANLY
leads LADY FARTHINGALE *to the other.*]

BEAU.

[*To* MARIANA.] May I have the delight of leading you
out in the dance?

MARIANA.

I fear, Mr. Brummel, you will find me but a poor dancer.

BEAU.

I know you dance well or I should not have asked you.
I have watched you. One must always judge for oneself.

[*He leads* MARIANA *to the head, opposite the*
PRINCE. *They dance an old-fashioned
quadrille, the end of which is a deep curtsy
from the ladies and bow from the men.
The* PRINCE *then goes up to center door and
out through the hall with* MRS. ST. AUBYN.]

[61]

BEAU BRUMMEL

PRINCE.

Egad! Poor Beau! Your charms have made me false to my friend.

MRS. ST. AUBYN.

Ah! But I fear Your Royal Highness is fickle, and may be false to me, too.

PRINCE.

Zounds! I could only be that by being false to myself.

> [*They are now out of sight. The* DUCHESS *had joined* BEAU *and* MARIANA, *and* LADY FARTHINGALE, LORD MANLY. *The two latter now curtsy and bow and exit through center door and go down the hall.*]

DUCHESS.

I really think it gives one more éclat to dance with Mr. Brummel than to dance with the Prince.

BEAU.

[*Quite sincerely.*] I really think it does.

> [*The* DUCHESS *and* MR. SHERIDAN *then bow and also go out at center door, meeting* VINCENT, *who bows to them in a most exaggerated way and then comes down toward the* BEAU *and* MARIANA. BEAU *bows in courtly fashion and also goes out through center door, so* VINCENT *and* MARIANA *are left alone.* MARIANA *is a charming type of a young English girl, dressed in white, her hair in soft ringlets, with a wreath of tiny rosebuds.*]

VINCENT.

This is the proudest moment of my life! He had heard of me; he recognized me at once, Mariana.

BEAU BRUMMEL

MARIANA.

[*Quizzically.*] Of course, papa, he had read your name on his buttons.

VINCENT.

You are mistaken, my dear; I am not a tailor, I am a cloth merchant. Did you notice how cordial His Royal Highness was? [*Regretfully.*] I was too stiff with him, much too stiff, but Mr. Brummel would have it so.

MARIANA.

[*Still trying to make a jest of it.*] Quite right, papa; you needed your dignity and His Royal Highness did not.

VINCENT.

Think, Mariana, what a difference to-day from yesterday. Yesterday I was Vincent, of the City—to-night, I am Vincent, of the Court. It is a proud position, my dear; think of it, Holiver Vincent, the Prince's friend! No more "The Hoak, the Hash, and the Bonny Hivy Tree." No more "A Weary Lot Is Thine, Fair Maid." [*Imitates the playing of a piano.*] No more going to sleep after dinner. No, my dear, we'll read our names every morning, several times over, in the Court Journal. It'll be a staggerer for your Aunt Jane at 'Oundsditch.

MARIANA.

[*Sadly.*] I think, for my part, we are very well as we are, and very happy. And I like the old songs, and I like my old father just as he is.

VINCENT.

Pooh! My child, I am ambitious and if you marry the Beau, in a year from now, I may wear a coronet—a coronet.

[*Makes a gesture as though placing a coronet on head.*]

MARIANA.

Uneasy lies the head that wears a crown, papa, and how

[63]

much are you going to give for the coronet? Anybody can buy one nowadays. Give your money for it by all means— but not your daughter's happiness.

> [*Crossing and going up toward center as though to end the discussion.*]

VINCENT.
[*Follows her and speaks pleadingly.*] Mariana, I have been a kind father to you. My heart is set upon the accomplishment of this thing. You have ever been a dutiful child.

MARIANA.
[*Turning quickly.*] And you shall ever find me so. But I hold, papa, that a woman's heart alone should guide a woman's choice.

VINCENT.
[*Turns away vexed.*] Yes, I know—but——

MARIANA.
Still, my affection for you shall largely influence my decision. Go, my ambitious father. [*Goes to him and puts her hands on his shoulders.*] I will see what I can do to win the coronet for your head.

VINCENT.
[*Delightedly kisses her forehead.*] That's a good child.
> [*He goes up and out through center door.*]

MARIANA.
If I can only tear the arrow from my heart. [*Walks slowly up and down.*] No dream of greatness, no wish even of my father's, should for one instant weaken my devotion to Reginald if I could believe him true to me. But he has ceased to write; I hear of him only in social dissipation. He is gay and merry, and Mariana is forgotten. Since I cannot be happy, there is only my dear old father to be pleased. And yet—and yet——

BEAU BRUMMEL

[*Starts and turns as* BEAU, *the* DUCHESS *and* MR. VINCENT *enter from the center door.*]

DUCHESS.

[*As she comes gaily down.*] Ma mie, you are very fortunate, I vow—you will be the talk of the town to-morrow—to have pirouetted with our Beau here. 'Tis no small favor I assure you—and one his Beauship has never yet bestowed upon his doting Duchess—you naughty, naughty Beau. [*Shakes her fan at* BEAU.] And I must say, *ma mie*, you comported yourself right well, right limber and nimbly for a débutante. Though I am no bad executante on the tips of my toes myself, i' faith.

[*Gives a little pas seul.*]

BEAU.

[*Putting up glasses and looking at her critically.*] Ah, Duchess, all you need is a ballet skirt and a tambourine. But, Egad, we forgot the Prince—the Merchant Prince—we have just left the title. Permit me, my dear Duchess, to present to you the money. Mr. Oliver Vincent—Her Grace, the Duchess of Leamington.

DUCHESS.

[*As she curtsies to* VINCENT, *who bows very low.*] Deuce take me, Mr. Brummel, have you ever known me to refuse a presentation to money?

BEAU.

No, my dear Duchess, and I have known you to become very familiar with it at the card-table without even a formal introduction.

DUCHESS.

Beau, I vow you're a brute.

[*She crosses to* VINCENT *and they go up a little.*]

BEAU.

[*Crossing to* MARIANA.] You hear that, Mariana. I am a brute, 'tis true, and I am looking forward to a con-

[65]

junction of Beauty and the Beast. [*Turning to the*
DUCHESS.] Duchess, shall Sir Money conduct you to the
card-room?

DUCHESS.

[*Smiling at Vincent.*] With pleasure, if he'll stay there
with me.

BEAU.

No fear of that, for your Grace is sure to put him in
your pocket.

DUCHESS.

Incorrigible! Come, Mr. Vincent, your arm, your arm;
fore Gad, we are routed.

[*Takes* VINCENT'S *arm, they turn to go.*]

BEAU.

[*Stopping them.*] One moment, my dear Vincent. [BEAU
bows to DUCHESS, *who joins* MARIANA, *and they stand
talking, while* BEAU *speaks to* VINCENT.] My valet has
neglected placing my purse in my pocket, and I am going
to allow you the privilege of lending me five hundred
guineas before you run away with the Duchess.

VINCENT.

[*Heartily.*] Certainly, my dear Mr. Brummel, certainly,
sir, take ten—— [*Puts his hand in his pocket.*]

BEAU.

[*With a look of horror.*] Not here, my good sir, not here—
in the card-room.

VINCENT.

[*Going up to the* DUCHESS.] My arm, madam, my purse
and myself are entirely at your service.

DUCHESS.

[*Taking his arm.*] I only need one of them; but come,
come, I see you are quite a courtier. *Au revoir*, Beau.
[*To Mariana, as she waves her a kiss.*] *Ma chere !*

BEAU BRUMMEL

[*Curtsies to the* BEAU, *waves her hand airily to* MARIANA *and goes off with* VINCENT.]

B E A U .
Your most humble and devoted slave, Duchess.

M A R I A N A .
You do not follow the cards, Mr. Brummel?

B E A U .
They are too fickle; I am always unlucky.

M A R I A N A .
Unlucky at cards, lucky in love——
　　　[*Stops abruptly, vexed that she has mentioned
　　　　the word love.*]

B E A U .
That is why I am here.

M A R I A N A .
[*A little coquettishly.*] Well, what sort of a hand shall I
deal you?

B E A U .
[*With great meaning.*] Yours!

M A R I A N A .
[*With equal meaning.*] Are diamonds trumps?

B E A U .
[*Reproachfully.*] No. Hearts!

M A R I A N A .
[*Lightly.*] I haven't one in the pack.

B E A U .
Nay, but you deal your cards badly.

M A R I A N A .
That is because I have chosen Nature, not Art, to be
my mistress.

[67]

BEAU BRUMMEL

BEAU.

By my manners! I've a mind to bring Dame Nature into fashion again.

MARIANA.

Then there's not a woman here could show her face.

BEAU.

But you. And if you would deign to be seen always on my arm——

MARIANA.

Mercy! Mr. Brummel, I fear you would wear me as you do your coat, and throw me aside when I'm wrinkled.

BEAU.

[*With a shudder.*] Don't mention wrinkles; they give me the jaundice.

MARIANA.

[*Seriously.*] I cannot but remember that only one short week ago every bench in the Mall, every lady's tea-table, every *entr'acte* of the play was the occasion for reportings of Mr. Brummel's fancy for the Hon. Mrs. St. Aubyn.

BEAU.

You cannot imagine I have not favored some woman more than others. Mrs. St. Aubyn was clever and amused me. We passed our time in laughter, not in loving.

[MRS. ST. AUBYN, *who has entered at back, hears this last remark.*]

MRS. ST. AUBYN.

I fear I am *malapropos*, but I will be deaf and blind.

[*She comes down the center, while there also enters at center door* VINCENT, SHERIDAN, LADY FARTHINGALE *and the* DUCHESS.]

MARIANA.

It would be a pity, madam, to destroy two faculties which serve you to such good purpose.

[68]

BEAU BRUMMEL

[Crosses and passes MRS. ST. AUBYN *with a slight bend of her head and joins* VINCENT.]

BEAU.

Oh, that's very good. [*To* MRS. ST. AUBYN *as he crosses to her.*] Don't you think that's very good?

[They stand together, apparently talking, MRS. ST. AUBYN *very angrily.*]

VINCENT.

[*To* MARIANA.] A most bewitching woman that, but I'm sorry she would insist upon hunting Mr. Brummel, for I knew you wouldn't want to be interrupted. I did all I could with politeness. I took her to every other room before this.

*[*MARIANA *and* VINCENT *go out at center door, as* LORD MANLY *comes rushing on, almost running into them.*]

LORD MANLY.

[*He is a fop of the period, and quite a little the worse for drink.*] My dear Beau! My dear Beau! [*A little louder.* BEAU *pays no attention to him.*] My dear Beau! [*Still louder.* BEAU *finally looks at him.*] Lord Crawlings is cheating at the card-table. It is a fact. He has cards up his sleeve. What shall I do?

BEAU.

Cheating at the card-table?

LORD MANLY.

Yes; he has cards up his sleeve.

BEAU.

[*Thoughtfully.*] Cards up his sleeve!

LORD MANLY.

Yes. What shall I do?

BEAU.

Well, if he has cards up his sleeve, bet on him.

[69]

BEAU BRUMMEL

LORD MANLY.

[*With a blank stare.*] Oh—thank you.

> [*He joins* LADY FARTHINGALE *and offers her a chair, which she refusing, they stand conversing with other guests.*]

LADY FARTHINGALE.

If Mr. Brummel marries Miss Vincent he'll have no more difficulty in paying for his clothes, though I hear he's sadly in debt now.

SHERIDAN.

Poor Beau! He will never be able to forget the old gentleman's cloth; it will be like riding to wealth on a clothes-horse.

DUCHESS.

[*Who has been looking down the hall.*] Lord, Mr. Sheridan! They are starting for supper. You can do as you please, but I want an oyster.

> [SHERIDAN *and* DUCHESS *go off at center door, followed by* LADY FARTHINGALE, LORD MANLY *and other guests.*]

MRS. ST. AUBYN.

[*To* BEAU, *who was starting to go.*] I insist upon a few words with you.

BEAU.

Your wishes are my commands.

> [*He is now standing in the door center so he can look down the hall.* MRS. ST. AUBYN *is walking angrily back and forth.*]

MRS. ST. AUBYN.

I found myself quite *de trop* when I entered the room a few minutes ago.

BEAU.

You speak of impossibilities.

[70]

BEAU BRUMMEL

MRS. ST. AUBYN.
Pray, spare me; I overheard your last speech.

BEAU.
You mean you listened to what I said.

MRS. ST. AUBYN.
Well, if I did—I begin to see through you now.

BEAU.
Happy me!

MRS. ST. AUBYN.
Did you think me blind when you presented these Vincents to the Prince?

BEAU.
[*Bowing to some imaginary guests down the hall.*] How do you do? Who could think those eyes blind?

MRS. ST. AUBYN.
You presented me to the Prince, not for my own sake, but for yours. 'Twas a pleasant way to be rid of me.

BEAU.
No way with such a destination could possibly be pleasant.

MRS. ST. AUBYN.
You have puffed the Prince with the conceit that he is driving you out of my affections against your will. Suppose he were to know the truth?

BEAU.
Royal personages are so rarely told the truth that if he did hear it he would not recognize it. How do you do! [*Again bowing to some imaginary person.*]

MRS. ST. AUBYN.
What would become of his friendship for you, do you think, and what would you do without it?

[71]

BEAU BRUMMEL

BEAU.

He would have my sincere sympathy.

MRS. ST. AUBYN.

Suppose I were to inform him?

BEAU.

[*Again bowing.*] How do you do, my dear Lady Betty; how do you do? Yes, presently—with great pleasure—h'm. [*Turning and apparently paying attention to* MRS. ST. AUBYN *for the first time.*] My dear Horatia would not be so foolish as to ruin herself. Would the Prince, do you think, still care for you if he thought I no longer admired you? He affects you now for the same reason he wears my coats, because I have made you as I made them—the Fashion.

MRS. ST. AUBYN.

[*Triumphantly.*] But there's something that binds one faster to a man than the button of a coat. There is, my dear Beau, such a thing as marriage.

BEAU.

Oh, yes, to be sure! There, my dear madam, I bow to your vast experience, [MRS. ST. AUBYN *makes an impatient movement*] but when it comes to a question of the Prince's wedding coat, I fear you will find the buttons are sewed on with a very light thread.

MRS. ST. AUBYN.

There you are wrong. You seem to forget, my dear Beau, that the Prince already dotes on me. We are both playing a little game—you and I—but I am persuaded I shall win, for I stake on a heart.

[*Sweeps past* BEAU *with a superb gesture, toward the left.*]

BEAU.

[*Very quietly.*] Your fortune will turn, for you stake on a knave.

[72]

BEAU BRUMMEL

MRS. ST. AUBYN.

What will take my knave when the king is out of the pack?

BEAU.

Why, then, I think a queen might turn up.

[*Before* MRS. ST. AUBYN *can crush him with the reply that is on her lips* VINCENT *enters.*]

VINCENT.

Ah, 'ere you are, my dear Mr. Brummel; you are losing your supper and Mrs. St. Aubyn, too, is depriving the feast of its most brilliant hornament.

BEAU.

Yes, truly, it is too selfish of Mrs. St. Aubyn. Mr. Vincent, Mrs. St. Aubyn must permit you to conduct her to the supper room.

MRS. ST. AUBYN.

[*Sarcastically.*] Surely, Mr. Vincent did not do *me* the honor of leaving the table to search me out.

VINCENT.

Fore Gad, madam, though I did see a vacant seat next His Royal Highness, in truth I came to look for my daughter.

BEAU.

Mrs. St. Aubyn will hardly permit the chair which awaits her next to the Prince to remain vacant. [*Takes* MRS. ST. AUBYN'S *hand and hands her with great "empressement" to* VINCENT.] Meanwhile, Mr. Vincent, I will go through the rooms for your daughter.

[MRS. ST. AUBYN *stops, gives* BEAU *a look, is about to make a scene, then thinks better of it and lets* VINCENT *lead her from the room.*]

BEAU.

You amused me once, but you do so no longer. No,

you're clever; yes, you are clever, and you dress to perfection, but Mariana has all your charms and more—a heart. Horatia St. Aubyn, your day in the world is waning; Mariana's reign begins. I will go and inform her so. She cannot be insensible to my regard, to my love, for, strange to say, I begin to think I do love her. Yes, I believe I do. [*Quite seriously.*] And I think I love her madly—yes, I do, I love her madly.

> [*Stands for a moment in deep thought, then walks slowly off through center door down the hall.* MARIANA *enters from door down right from reception room. She has a note in her hand.*]

MARIANA.

Kathleen has conveyed to me my own letter to Reginald unopened. She says he has left his lodgings, and his landlady does not know when he will return. I am afraid men are not what they are represented to be.

> [*Sits down in chair near the door at right.* LORD MANLY *comes on through hall and center door. He is slightly intoxicated.*]

LORD MANLY.

Ah! Miss Vincent! What happiness.

MARIANA.

[*Annoyed.*] Here's another!

LORD MANLY.

Won't you drink something? I mean eat something?

MARIANA.

[*Not looking at him.*] Thank you, I care for nothing! There can be no mistake; Kathleen vowed she delivered the letters.

LORD MANLY.

You won't eat, and you won't drink—most 'straordinary! What *will* you do?

" *I begin to think I do love her.   Yes, I believe I do—and I think*
I love her madly—yes, I do, I love her madly."

BEAU BRUMMEL

MARIANA.

I will dispense with your society, sir. [*As she rises, she looks at him.*] I do believe he is intoxicated.

LORD MANLY.

She's coy! She's coy! No, fair creature, I have follolled—follolled—I have follolled—most 'straordinary I can't say follolled—I have follolled you from room to room to find you.

MARIANA.

And having found me, you may leave me, sir!

LORD MANLY.

Leave you! Never! Never will I stir from this sacred spot. [*In his endeavor to stand quite still, staggers and almost falls over.*] I mean the sacred spot where you are. Miss Vincent, I adore you! Fact. All you do, I see through rosy-colored glasses.

MARIANA.

Wine-colored glasses you mean, sir. Let me pass!

LORD MANLY.

No, fair tantalizer. [*Nods his head with great satisfaction.*] Good word—tantalizer. I will speak; my heart is full.

MARIANA.

There can be no doubt about the fulness.

LORD MANLY.

Here on my knees [*looks at knees*]—Egad, look at my knees. I have four knees instead of two knees—but, no matter—here on all my knees [*kneels, almost falling*] I will pour out——

MARIANA.

More liquor, sir. You do not need it.

LORD MANLY.

You cannot ignore me, my love, my passion, my *adorashion*—I mean adoration, Miss Vincent—I——

[75]

BEAU BRUMMEL

[BEAU *has come on through center door. Unperceived he comes down, takes* LORD MANLY *by the ear, making him rise and stagger back.*]

BEAU.

My dear Miss Vincent, how unfortunately unconventional.

LORD MANLY.

Mr. Brummel, sir, you are no gentleman.

BEAU.

My good fellow, you are no judge.

LORD MANLY.

My honor, sir, my honor!

BEAU.

Fiddlesticks! Come trot away, trot away. You may apologize to Miss Vincent to-morrow.

LORD MANLY.

You apologize to me now, sir.

BEAU.

I never had occasion to do such a thing in my life. [*Walks up and looks off down the hall.*] Now trot away; I think I see the Prince approaching.

LORD MANLY.

Proach aprincing!—I mean Prince approaching. Miss Vincent, it is with deep regret I say adieu!
[*He stumbles to door at right and goes off.*]

BEAU.

[*Coming down and offering* MARIANA *a chair. She sits.*] I heartily congratulate you, my dear Miss Vincent, on having escaped a scene. Nothing but the regard I bear you could have persuaded me to so nearly incur a possible fracas. Lord Manly was born with a silver spoon in his mouth, and he has thought it necessary to keep that spoon

[76]

" *I begin to belicve in you.*"

full ever since. But now that we have found one another, may I not be permitted to continue the conversation where it was broken off? I desire to speak with you seriously. I wish to make a confession. I want to tell you what perhaps you know—when I first sought your hand, I did not bring my heart. I admired you, 'tis true, but I did not love you— not then—not madly! I was—I am so deeply in debt, so hemmed in by my creditors, so hard pressed on every side, it was necessary for me to do something to find the wherewithal to satisfy their just demands, or sink under my misfortunes and give up forever the life of the world which had become my very breath and being. The one means at my disposal to free myself from my difficulties was a marriage. I knew your fortune and I sought you out. The admiration I entertained for you the first few days deepened into esteem and finally expanded into love—mad love! That is why I have rehearsed this to you. At first it was your fortune which allured me—but now it is yourself!

MARIANA.

Mr. Brummel!

BEAU.

Yet, were you penniless I would not wed you.

MARIANA.

[*Rising in astonishment.*] Mr. Brummel!

BEAU.

Because I would not drag you down to share this miser-able, uncertain lot of mine. No! I would seek you once to tell you of my love, and then step aside out of your path, and never cross it again. I would not willingly, purposely encompass your unhappiness.

MARIANA.

[*Slowly.*] I begin to believe in you.

[77]

BEAU BRUMMEL

BEAU.

I remember no other word that you have spoken. May I have the delight of pressing my very unworthy lips to your very dear hand?

[MARIANA *is about to give* BEAU *her hand, then suddenly withdraws it.*]

MARIANA.

I think, Mr. Brummel, I would rather you did not.

BEAU.

[*Thoughtfully.*] I believe you are right. Yes, I am quite sure you are. Thank you. You have saved me from doing something very commonplace.

MARIANA.

You are not angry, sir?

BEAU.

I believe it is exactly fifteen years since I last lost my temper—but, Mariana, I still await your answer. It is a new sensation for Brummel to be kept waiting.

MARIANA.

Will you leave me, sir, to consider my decision? I pray you, Mr. Brummel, give me a few moments here—alone.

[*She motions toward recess farthest down stage and crosses toward it.*]

BEAU.

I would refuse you nothing. I will await your pleasure in this other recess, and seek you here in five slow minutes.

[*He motions toward the recess the farthest up stage and with a low bow to* MARIANA *goes in and draws the curtain.*]

MARIANA.

[*Stands holding the curtain which closes the recess where*

[78]

BEAU BRUMMEL

she is standing.] I cannot bring myself to say yes to him, although a certain sympathy pleads in his behalf, and joins with pride to prompt me against Reginald, who has neglected me. Why has he not replied to my letters? 'Tis very soon to be forgotten! Oh, Reginald, to be absent when most I needed you. You are no better than the men of the world. Father is right. Mr. Brummel shall have his answer. [*The* PRINCE *and* MRS. ST. AUBYN *enter at center door, so much engrossed in each other they do not see* MARIANA.] Oh, how provoking!
[MARIANA *hides in recess and draws the curtain.*]

BEAU.

[*Who has also looked out at that moment.*] How very annoying! I shall have to play Patience on a window-seat and wait.

MRS. ST. AUBYN.

Yes. I must own to you my sentiments toward Mr. Brummel are greatly altered. Until I met you—can you believe it?—I positively thought him a man of some parts.

BEAU.

[*From the window.*] Really, really!

PRINCE.

Goddess! Of course, he has been much with me, and naturally smacks somewhat of my wit.

BEAU.

Ah, that's very good! Very good!

MRS. ST. AUBYN.

But only as a false echo does, for he has none of your delicate pleasantry.

BEAU.

No, thank goodness, I haven't.

MRS. ST. AUBYN.

He mimics you in dress, in everything, but, then, you know, he never had your figure.

[79]

BEAU BRUMMEL

[The PRINCE *and* MRS. ST. AUBYN *go toward middle recess and seat themselves.]*

BEAU.

Heaven forbid!

MRS. ST. AUBYN.

He really has no taste.

PRINCE.

He showed that when he chose Miss Vincent for his marked attention.

MRS. ST. AUBYN.

And do you think so, too? Why, I know Miss Vincent is an insignificant little thing, whose name has never been associated with any gentleman of quality, but though without mind or manners, she has money, sir. She dresses like a guy, but her clothes, like the clouds, have a silver lining.

MARIANA.

[With a hasty look out of the curtain.] I wish I could escape by the window.

BEAU.

I've half a mind to crawl out of the window, but I might be observed. There's no resource but to try to go asleep.

PRINCE.

You are a flatterer and a coquette.

MRS. ST. AUBYN.

No; only a woman—and under a spell.

PRINCE.

Damme, that sounds very fine. I should like——

MRS. ST. AUBYN.

Well?

PRINCE.

I should like to be one of those little words that kiss your lips and die.

[80]

BEAU BRUMMEL

BEAU.

One of my pet speeches—number five

MRS. ST. AUBYN.

Beware, sir, let me warn you—remember, I have been married once already.

PRINCE.

Fore Gad, madam, I wish that you would marry twice.

MRS. ST. AUBYN.

Never! Now! To be sure, I once thought there was something like love engendered in me by Mr. Brummel, but now I know it was not real love; it was only a shadow.

PRINCE.

Why do you think that?

> [*At this moment* VINCENT *enters from the center door. All the curtains of the different windows are drawn so he can see no one.*]

VINCENT.

I cannot keep away any longer; she's been sensible and accepted him, or they'd have been gone long before this. [MRS. ST. AUBYN *moves the curtain a little, with a slight exclamation.*] There they are in the recess behind the curtain. Oh, he's clever—Mr. Brummel—very clever.

MRS. ST. AUBYN.

I tremble to acknowledge, even to myself, the dictates of my own heart. Ah, sir, I conceive you know only too well who reigns there now.

VINCENT.

[*Who apparently cannot hear.*] I should just like to hear a word to see how the great Mr. Brummel makes love. I wonder would it be wrong now to listen a bit? Why should it be—am I not her father? It's my duty, and I will. [*Comes further down and listens.*]

BEAU BRUMMEL

PRINCE.

Siren! You make me drunk with joy!

MRS. ST. AUBYN.

No; let me recover myself. You have bewitched me, sir. I must resist your fascinations and not forget the difference in our rank. Fashion would condemn me.

PRINCE.

Damn Fashion!

VINCENT.

Oh! Mr. Brummel a-damning Fashion. How he loves her! How he loves her.

MRS. ST. AUBYN.

Ah! sir, we women are so frail, so easily beguiled!

PRINCE.

[*Falling on his knees.*] By heaven, I will not lose you!

VINCENT.

[*Joyfully.*] He's on his knees! He's on his knees!

PRINCE.

Superb! sumptuous! beautiful woman!

[*Kisses her hand.*]

VINCENT.

He's kissing her! He's kissing her!

PRINCE.

I swear I will marry you!

VINCENT.

[*Who can restrain himself no longer, rushes forward and draws curtain aside.*] And so you shall! Bless you my—— [*Sees the* PRINCE *and* MRS. ST. AUBYN. *Falls back.*] Oh, Lord! The Prince!

[*All guests enter at center door.*]

PRINCE.

[*Rising, indignantly.*] What do you mean, sir. Con-

" Wales, will you ring the bell ? "

BEAU BRUMMEL

found your damned impudence. Will some one show this gentleman——

BEAU.
[*Who has come slowly down.*] Oh, take his blessing; it won't hurt you.

PRINCE.
Damn his blessing.

BEAU.
Be composed, my dear Wales, or you'll make a fool of yourself.

PRINCE.
[*Too exasperated to take from* BEAU *what he usually thinks all right.*] Oh, I am tired of your deuced impertinence, too Beau. Step aside, step aside!

BEAU.
[*Slowly handing his snuff-box to the* PRINCE.] My dear Wales, first you lose your equilibrium, and now you lose your temper. Take a little snuff.

PRINCE.
Damn your snuff! [*Knocks snuff-box out of* BEAU'S *hand.*]

BEAU.
[*Puts up his glass and looks quietly at him.*] Very bad manners, very bad.   I shall have to order my carriage. Wales, will you ring the bell?

> [*Everybody is aghast at* BEAU's *daring. The* PRINCE *stands petrified.* BEAU *holds out his hand to* MARIANA, *who has been standing in the recess half fainting. She comes forward, bows low to the* PRINCE, *and backs to the door, followed by her father, who is pitifully dejected. The curtain comes down as* BEAU, *with a last look at the* PRINCE *through his glass, turns and walks toward the door.*]

THE END OF THE SECOND ACT.

[83]

THE THIRD ACT

THE THIRD ACT

*The Mall, St. James Park, the great promenade where
every day all London walks. There are benches on
each side of the stage under the trees. At the back
ladies and gentlemen can be seen walking.*

> [MORTIMER *comes on from right-hand side,
> walks up and down impatiently. After a
> little* KATHLEEN *appears in a great hurry.*]

KATHLEEN.

Oh! You're there, are you?

MORTIMER.

[*Indignantly.*] Am I here? You're half an hour late.

KATHLEEN.

[*Airily.*] Well, what do you expect? Aren't I a woman?
Say, what's the matter with your face; you have an awful
gloomy expression of countenance?

MORTIMER.

[*Laughing.*] You little minx. Well, how goes it?

KATHLEEN.

[*Crossing to bench and sitting down.*] Why, bad. I can't
for the life of me keep one lie from spoiling the other. Say,
is all this true about Mr. Brummel and the Prince?

[87]

BEAU BRUMMEL

MORTIMER.

Yes. We've quarreled.

KATHLEEN.

And did the Prince cut ye's?

MORTIMER.

No; we cut the Prince, and on account of you Vincents, too. The Prince is deuced put out with Mr. Brummel, [*crosses to bench and sits*] so Bendon told me. It's all abroad, and I left a swarm of creditors at the house, and, worse still, there are two bailiffs after him. [KATHLEEN *gives an exclamation of horror.*] We must hurry on this marriage, Kathleen, or you and I'll be ruined. We must take pains to keep Mr. Brummel and his nephew apart, for he's that partial to him there's no telling what he mightn't do if he was to discover Miss Mariana and Mr. Reginald were lovers.

KATHLEEN.

And we must see to it that Miss Mariana and Mr. Reginald don't meet, else he'd explain how he'd never received any of her letters. I kept them all carefully, for I thought it might comfort him to read 'em after she was married to Mr. Brummel. But I must be off. [*Rises.*] Good morning, me Lud.   [*Makes very deep curtsy.*]

MORTIMER.

[*Bowing very low.*] Till this evening, me Lady.

KATHLEEN.

Till this evening.

    [*Turns to go out and meets* REGINALD *face to face.*]

REGINALD.

Ah! Kathleen, where have you been this last week?

KATHLEEN.

[*Is very much perturbed;* MORTIMER *has retreated to the back of the Mall and then disappeared.*] Here, sir, here.

[88]

BEAU BRUMMEL

REGINALD.
Will your mistress be in the Park this morning?

KATHLEEN.
No, sir; she left town to-day, sir.

REGINALD.
[*A little wistfully.*] Was she—in good spirits, Kathleen?

KATHLEEN.
Oh, beautiful, sir! She skipt with joy.

REGINALD.
[*Gives* KATHLEEN *money and then slowly walks away.*]
I cannot understand it. I am sure there is some mistake.

KATHLEEN.
[*Looking at the coin disdainfully.*] That's mighty small
pay for a mighty big lie. Bad cess to him.

> [*She walks off at the right with a toss of her
> head. As she disappears* REGINALD *comes
> down as though to call her back, but she has
> gone, and he turns to see* MORTIMER.]

REGINALD.
Ah, Mortimer, is Mr. Brummel well?

MORTIMER.
[*Very respectfully, hat in hand.*] No, sir. Not at all, sir.
He can see no one, sir.

REGINALD.
But he will see me?

MORTIMER.
Excuse me, sir, but he especially mentioned your name,
sir; he could not even see you.

REGINALD.
Will he not be in the Mall this morning?

[89]

BEAU BRUMMEL

MORTIMER.

No, oh, no, sir.

REGINALD.

Well, tell him I will visit him to-morrow.

[REGINALD *goes off down path to the right.*]

MORTIMER.

That was a tight squeeze. I expect him here any moment. I must see him and warn him of the bailiffs, if he only arrives before they do.

[MORTIMER *goes off hurriedly by a path to the left. BEAU enters from the lower left-hand side and walks slowly to the center, followed by MORTIMER. MORTIMER seems quite out of breath. BEAU is dressed in dark green silk knee breeches, green coat, black silk stockings, buckled shoes, frilled shirt and neckcloth, wears two fobs, carries cane with eye-glass in the top, gray high hat of the period, yellow waistcoat, yellow gloves, large red boutonniere.*]

MORTIMER.

Mr. Brummel, sir!

[BEAU *starts, turns, lifts cane slowly, looks at MORTIMER through glass on top, then turns away and continues his walk.*]

MORTIMER.

[*Very deferentially, but firmly.*] Mr. Brummel, sir!

BEAU.

[*Without turning.*]   I think there is some mistake.

MORTIMER.

Excuse me, sir, but I *must* speak to you.

BEAU.

You forget, Mortimer, servants in the street are like

[90]

BEAU BRUMMEL

children at the table, they may be seen, but must not be heard.

MORTIMER.

I have not forgotten, sir, but this is serious.

BEAU.

Serious! then it is sure to be unpleasant—wait till I take some snuff.

> [*Takes snuff very quietly and with much cere-mony, replaces box, then nods to* MORTIMER *and listens.*]

MORTIMER.

Sir, your quarrel with the Prince is already common talk.

BEAU.

[*Brushing a little snuff off his ruffles.*] Ah, poor Wales!

MORTIMER.

There was a crowd of creditors at your door when I left, sir.

BEAU.

That is neither new nor serious.

MORTIMER.

But they were angry and would not go away.

BEAU.

Why did you not send them off?

MORTIMER.

Sir, we've been sending them off for the past two years, and now—they won't *be* sent. Besides, sir, there are two bailiffs who swore they'd have you if they had to take you in the Mall.

BEAU.

Impossible!

MORTIMER.

I fear not, sir; one is from Mr. Abrahams.

BEAU BRUMMEL

BEAU.

Here? In the Mall? I would rather perish. There is no help for it. [*To himself.*] I must make a shield of my marriage. I blush to do it, for it would seem to leave a blot upon my love for Mariana, but a blot upon that love is better than a blot upon the name of Brummel, the name she is to wear. [*Aloud to Mortimer.*] Mortimer!

MORTIMER.

Yes, sir.

BEAU.

You must hasten back and meet them, these dogs of bailiffs; you must prevent them by telling them of my marriage to the daughter of Mr. Oliver Vincent. That prospect should satisfy them. Promise them all they demand and added interest. [BEAU *starts to go off at the right-hand side,* MORTIMER *also moves off to the left.*] Promise them everything. [MORTIMER *stops and bows respectfully, then starts again.* BEAU *moves on a few paces then stops again.*] Promise them anything.

> [MORTIMER *again stops and bows.* BEAU *moves on again and* MORTIMER *also starts again to go.* BEAU *stops suddenly.*]

BEAU.

And, Mortimer! [MORTIMER *stops, comes back a few steps.*] You must not go unrewarded; [MORTIMER *looks pleased and expectant*] promise yourself something!

> [BEAU *walks slowly off at the right-hand side and* MORTIMER, *with a low bow, replaces his hat and goes quickly off at the left side.*]

MORTIMER.

[*As he exits.*] Yes, sir!

> [VINCENT *and* MARIANA *enter from the upper left-hand entrance.* MARIANA *is dressed*

[92]

simply but prettily in a light flowered silk gown, poke bonnet, parasol.]

VINCENT.

We'll be sure to meet him here somewhere. You must do it all, Mariana. He was just as haughty with me last night after we left Carlton House as he always was. You wouldn't have thought he had just sacrificed himself for me.

MARIANA.

Sacrificed himself for *you*, papa?

VINCENT.

Isn't it sacrificing himself for him to give up his position in the world? And isn't that what he has done to resent your father's insult?

MARIANA.

[*Trying to lighten the seriousness of the situation.*] I fancied he did it partly on my account, papa.

VINCENT.

Of course, you little rogue, it was for us both, but it's you alone who can repay him. He hasn't a penny and this rupture with the Prince has brought down all his creditors upon him. With the money your dowry will bring him [MARIANA *turns her head away, biting her lip*] he can pay off his creditors and defy the Prince. Without it he can do neither and is utterly ruined.

MARIANA.

I realize, father, that it is through us this sudden calamity has come upon Mr. Brummel. It was you, papa, who were to blame. Why did you bring down the curtain before the comedy was over?

VINCENT.

[*A little irritably.*] Come, come, Mariana, you have too teasing a temper.

BEAU BRUMMEL

MARIANA.

[*Seriously enough now.*] Ah, my dear father, I only
want to help you by making light of the matter. Come,
[*taking his arm and crossing slowly toward the right*] let
us find Mr. Brummel. I am not blind to the fact that it
was by protecting you and me he exposed himself to insult.
Well, he shall not suffer for it. Father, I promise you
that I will accept his hand.

VINCENT.

And I feel sure that it will mean happiness for you in the
end. Wait here [*seats* MARIANA *on bench at right*] a
moment, and I will return with Mr. Brummel.

[VINCENT *exits at the upper right-hand path.*]

MARIANA.

Yes, yes. I must hesitate no longer. I must think now
only of my father, and not remember Reginald, who has
neglected me. Gratitude and sympathy shall take the
place of love in my heart.

[MRS. ST. AUBYN *enters from right-hand entrance, dressed very exquisitely in white,
large white hat, carries a fan.*]

MRS. ST. AUBYN.

Ah, Miss Vincent! Is Mr. Brummel with you?

[*Makes a very slight curtsy.*]

MARIANA.

[*Rising and curtsying.*] No; my father.

MRS. ST. AUBYN.

And you have him to thank for the scene last evening.
It is he Mr. Brummel has to thank for the Prince's dis-
pleasure.

MARIANA.

[*Anxiously.*] Madam, and is the Prince still angry?

[94]

BEAU BRUMMEL

MRS. ST. AUBYN.

[*With great relish.*] He is furious and swears he will never forgive him. There is, I think, only one person who could influence him in Mr. Brummel's behalf, and that person—is—myself!

[*Crosses triumphantly in front of* MARIANA *with a sweep of her fan on the last word.*]

MARIANA.

[*Eagerly going a little toward her.*] Then, surely, you who have been such a good friend of Mr. Brummel will use your influence in his behalf. Indeed, if I am not wrong, it was through Mr. Brummel that you met the Prince. Your smoothing this quarrel, then, will be but a fair return to him.

MRS. ST. AUBYN.

You forget I am a woman of fashion. We take all we can get, but we never give anything. No, only on one condition shall I persuade the Prince to hold Mr. Brummel again in favor.

MARIANA.

[*With quiet scorn.*] Ah, I see, a condition. Then you women of the world condescend to sell, if you will not give.

MRS. ST. AUBYN.

[*Angrily.*] You would do better not to ruffle me. My condition is this: If you will promise to relinquish Mr. Brummel, I will make the Prince promise not to cut him, as he has sworn to do publicly to-day.

[*Looks triumphantly at* MARIANA, *then turns away as though to give her time to consider.*]

MARIANA.

I would I could accept this proposition, but I cannot, I cannot. 'Twould be the greatest injustice to Mr. Brummel. I must not forget that he did not hesitate to sacrifice him-

self for me and my father. I spoke to her of making him a return. Let me not shrink then from making as just a one myself. [*Then speaking to* MRS. ST. AUBYN, *who has turned toward* MARIANA.] What right have you to ask any one to give him up?

MRS. ST. AUBYN.

He sought my favors before you enticed him from me.

MARIANA.

[*Very quietly.*] I do not believe that.

MRS. ST. AUBYN.

[*Angrily.*] You are uncommonly insolent. [*Then changing her tone to one of condescension.*] Well, even if it were not so I should still have the right to ask you. You seem to forget the difference in our position.

> [*She sweeps past* MARIANA *with a grand air toward the right. At this moment* BEAU *enters from the right-hand side; he has over-heard the last speech. He crosses to the center, bowing to* MRS. ST. AUBYN *as he passes her, and with a very low bow to* MARIANA *says:*]

BEAU.

It is you, Mrs. St. Aubyn, who forget. It is greatly to the credit of Miss Vincent if she can overlook a difference your present conduct makes so very marked.

MRS. ST. AUBYN.

[*With a very low curtsy.*] I will repeat to you what I have just said to Miss Vincent.

BEAU.

[*Airily.*] Pray do not fatigue yourself, madam.

MRS. ST. AUBYN.

You will learn that I know how to remain a friend when

BEAU BRUMMEL

once I become one. I offered Miss Vincent the chance of regaining for you the Prince's friendship.

BEAU.

And your price?

MRS. ST. AUBYN.

[*In a low tone.*] Yourself.

BEAU.

[*To* MARIANA.] And you, you refused? [MARIANA *bows her head.*] It would have been most unflattering, madam, had Miss Vincent disposed of me so cheaply.

MRS. ST. AUBYN.

[*Who is now enraged almost beyond the bounds of endurance.*] Are you mad? Do you know to whom you are speaking? You are somewhat rash, sir. Discard me and the Prince shall know *all*.

BEAU.

He knows so very little at present, the knowledge of anything would be largely to his advantage. And yet—I cannot imagine you will tell him—*all*.

MRS. ST. AUBYN.

Your raillery is ill planned. A woman scorned——

BEAU.

Pray spare us, Mrs. St. Aubyn; you were never intended for tragedy—it does not become you—and it produces [*pause*]—wrinkles.

MRS. ST. AUBYN.

[*Has now recovered her composure.*] Mr. Brummel, I bid you adieu—you have taught me how to smile even when—tush—I am a woman of fashion! [*Crosses to left, passing* MARIANA.] Miss Vincent, I wish you joy. [*With an exaggerated deep curtsy.* MARIANA *curtsies. Looks off up the left path, calls:*] Manly—Lord Manly. [MANLY

comes on, raises hat, bows.]   Lord Manly—your arm—your arm.   [*They go off arm in arm.*]

MARIANA.
[*Sinking down on bench.*]   Your regard and protection leave me too much in your debt.

BEAU.
Pray let that debt weigh no more heavily on you than do my debts on me.   One smile of yours had overpaid me.

MARIANA.
If your creditors were as easily satisfied as you are, sir, I should be prodigal of my smiles.

BEAU.
[*Crossing to* MARIANA'S *side.*]   Ah, Mariana, if your smiles were the coinage, Egad, I think I should turn miser.

MARIANA.
You are not practical, sir.   I must make you so.

BEAU.
I am your slave and the chains I wear are no burden. May I indeed hope that you will accept my humble service? That you will be my wife?   [*Stands hat in hand.*]

MARIANA.
Yes, Mr. Brummel, I honor and respect you. [*Gives her hand to* BEAU.]   I will be your wife.

BEAU.
[*Kissing her hand.*]   And may I hope you will learn to love me a little?

MARIANA.
I do indeed hope so.   [*Aside.*]   Or make myself forget.

BEAU.
[*Putting on his hat with a buoyant gesture.*]   Come,

" If your creditors were as easily satisfied as you are, sir,
I should be prodigal of my smiles."

BEAU BRUMMEL

Mariana, [MARIANA *rises*] honor my arm—and we will
tell the whole world of our—of *my* happiness.

> [*They go off at left-hand path. Vincent enters
> from the right.*]

VINCENT.

I can't find him anywhere. I'm afraid he's hiding, poor
fellow, from those bailiffs, and doesn't dare show his face
lest he be taken. Where's Mariana? Has she changed
her mind and gone? No, she gave her promise she'd
accept him and I can trust to her word. I'll search for her
now and perhaps by so doing I may find him.

> [VINCENT *goes out by upper path, left-hand side.
> Two bailiffs enter from upper right-hand
> path. They are villainous-looking creatures;
> one limps—the other has a patch over one eye
> and both have very red noses; they are dressed
> in ragged clothes.*]

FIRST BAILIFF.

Our gentleman's so fine we mustn't bother our eyes
with winking or he'll slip through our fingers.

SECOND BAILIFF.

Not if I know it. This is the most fashionable affair
of my life. Look here—who's this?

> [*He points to the left-hand path. They both
> quickly withdraw behind a tree. BEAU
> enters from the left.*]

BEAU.

I'll leave her to inform her father. I must find Mortimer; he should have returned by now. What if he should
not have met those bailiffs—if they should still be at large.
Zounds!   [*He sits on bench at right.*]

FIRST BAILIFF.

[*In a low tone.*] That's him!

SECOND BAILIFF.

Lud—ain't he scrumptious! We ought to have a pair of silver sugar-tongs to take him with.

[*They come down, one behind the other.*]

FIRST BAILIFF.

Mr. Brummel, sir!

BEAU.

[*Looking up.*] The devil!

FIRST BAILIFF.

No, sir, the bailiff.

BEAU.

What is the difference?

[*The bailiffs look at one another in amazement.*]

FIRST BAILIFF.

We've been looking for you, sir.

BEAU.

I am so sorry you have put yourself to that trouble, and you must not speak to me here. Do you realize what you are doing? Suppose some one were to observe you. My valet will attend to you.

FIRST BAILIFF.

Oh, we'll take care of your valet later; it's you that we've got a couple of papers for this morning. I represent your landlord, sir!

[BEAU *lifts his cane with great deliberation and looks at him through glass.*]

BEAU.

Are you the best he can do?

FIRST BAILIFF.

You have lived in his house three years, and he considers it's time as how you paid a bit of rent.

BEAU BRUMMEL

BEAU.

[*As though to himself.*] The ungrateful wretch! The very fact of my having resided in his house should be more than sufficient remuneration.

SECOND BAILIFF.

[*Comes up in front of* BEAU, *while* FIRST BAILIFF *retires a little, shaking his head, as though completely puzzled.*]

And I am here for Mr. Abrahams and several other gentlemen.

BEAU.

You remind me of the person in the theatre whom they call the super, who represents the enemy on the march or the company in the ballroom. We will dispense with your company, sir.

FIRST BAILIFF.

[*Coming up again.*] That won't do, Mr. Brummel. You must pay, or come along with us.

[*Makes vague gesture of thumb over shoulder.*]

SECOND BAILIFF.

[*Making same gesture as he withdraws again.*] Yes, pay or come along with us.

BEAU.

You men must be mad; the Prince will be here presently, and I will speak to him. [*Rises.*]

FIRST BAILIFF.

[*Obsequiously.*] Oh, if His Royal Highness will help you, sir, of course, we won't press matters.

BEAU.

See that you do not. And now [*looking at them through his glass*] trot away, trot away, and walk in Fleet Street; the Mall is really no place for you.

[*He turns, lifts his boutonniere so he can inhale the perfume of the flowers, and then walks*

BEAU BRUMMEL

away with great deliberation. They stand staring after him for an instant, stupefied.]

FIRST BAILIFF.
We'll keep our eye on our gentleman, just the same. These little rumors about the Prince and him might be true after all, and if they are, why we won't walk in Fleet Street alone.

> [*He takes a black bottle out of his pocket, takes a drink and then hands it to the* SECOND BAILIFF, *who also takes a drink, then they go off in the same direction* BEAU *went. The* DUCHESS, LADY FARTHINGALE, LORD MANLY *and* SHERRY *come on from the left-hand path.* LORD MANLY *and* LADY FARTHINGALE *cross to the right-hand bench.* LADY FARTHINGALE *sits,* MANLY *stands by her side. Three ladies and gentlemen come on at the back and stand there, apparently chatting or listening to the* DUCHESS.]

DUCHESS.
Where can Beau have disappeared to? It's near time for the Prince to be out, and I wouldn't miss observing the meeting for worlds. Pray, Sherry, give us your opinion—will he cut him or not?

> [*The* DUCHESS *has been flying around looking for* BEAU *in every direction.*]

SHERIDAN.
Really, Duchess, I cannot say what the Prince will do. He's too great a fool for me to put myself in his place.

MANLY.
Damme, of course, he'll cut him, and, moreover, Beau deserves it.

SHERIDAN.
[*Decidedly.*] Then, for my part, I say, let's move on.

[102]

BEAU BRUMMEL

DUCHESS.

[*Equally decided.*] We'll do no such thing. We must see for ourselves, so that we can trust our own ears and know how to treat Mr. Brummel accordingly. Besides, if we observe it, we can inform others of the affair correctly, and there will be some merit in that.

[SHERIDAN *moves away to the right, with a shrug of his shoulders.*]

LADY FARTHINGALE.

Mr. Brummel will never be able to stand it if he's injured. I should not wonder now if he fainted!

DUCHESS.

Dear me, do you think so? [*Face falls as though disappointed.*] I don't know, I'm afraid not.

SHERIDAN.

[*Impatiently.*] He's more likely to resent any insult, I'm convinced.

DUCHESS.

[*Most excited, rushes to* LADY FARTHINGALE.] What! A duel! Oh, Lud, Lady Farthingale, only think—a duel! Deuce take it, where can Beau be? I'm afraid the Prince will arrive first.

SHERIDAN.

[*Sarcastically.*] My dear Duchess, prithee be calm; you are too great an enthusiast.

DUCHESS.

[*Looking off at the right.*] Here comes Mr. Brummel, I vow. Do you notice anything different in his manner of walking?

SHERIDAN.

[*Monocle in eye, looks off in direction* BEAU *is supposed to be.*] He seems to have the same number of legs as formerly. [*He crosses over to the left.*]

BEAU BRUMMEL

DUCHESS.

Oh, you may rail at me, Sherry, but it's no laughing matter for Mr. Brummel, I can tell you.

LADY FARTHINGALE.

[*Rising so she can see better.*] He's coming—he's coming!

DUCHESS.

Lud, we must not expose ourselves. We must at least feign utter ignorance of the affair. [BEAU *enters.*] Ah, Beau!   [*The ladies curtsy, men raise their hats.*]

BEAU.

Still loitering, Duchess? I was so afraid you would have returned home.   [*He joins* SHERRY *on the other side.*]

DUCHESS.

[*Aside to* LADY FARTHINGALE.] You hear? A hint for us to go, but he'll not hoodwink his Duchess. [*To* BEAU.] We were just going, but we'll rest a moment for another chat with you.

BEAU.

Too good of you, Duchess. Are you not afraid to risk your—what's that called, Sherry? [*Touching his cheek.*]

SHERRY.

[*Much embarrassed.*] Complexion.

BEAU.

Yes, your complexion in the sun.

> [*Chats with* SHERRY. DUCHESS, *very angry, does not know what to say until* LADY FARTHINGALE'S *speech gives her a chance to show her spitefulness.*]

LADY FARTHINGALE.

Here comes His Royal Highness!

BEAU BRUMMEL

DUCHESS.

[*Looking off at the right.*] The Prince! Is he truly? I didn't expect him this morning. Beau, the Prince is coming.

BEAU.

[*Indifferently.*] Is he really? Where's the music? In the play the Prince always comes on with music. Let's be going, Sherry, there's no music.

> [*Takes* SHERRY'S *arm and they move off to the left.*]

DUCHESS.

[*Meaningly.*] What, Beau, you wouldn't leave before His Royal Highness comes?

BEAU.

[*Seeing there is no escape, meets his fate gallantly.*] By my manners, no. Sherry, let us meet him.

> [*They turn and start to the right as the* PRINCE *enters with* MRS. ST. AUBYN *on his arm. The* DUCHESS *has retreated back to where* LADY FARTHINGALE *is standing.*]

DUCHESS.

The deuce, did you hear that Lady Farthingale?

> [BEAU *and* SHERRY *reach the center and stop. The* PRINCE *and* MRS. ST. AUBYN *pass directly by* BEAU, *although he stands hat in hand, and address* SHERRY. BEAU *replaces hat and listens with an amused expression.*]

PRINCE.

Sup with me to-night, Sherry, after the play. Mrs. St. Aubyn and the Duchess will be there with us, and, Egad, we'll make a night of it.

> [SHERRY *can only bow acquiescence and the* PRINCE *and* MRS. ST. AUBYN *move on a little way.* BEAU, *lifting his glass, looks after them and says to* SHERRY :]

[105]

BEAU BRUMMEL

BEAU.

Sherry, who's your fat friend?

[SHERRY *is divided between delight and amaze-*
ment at his daring and consternation at
thought of the consequences, and whispers in
BEAU'S *ear.*]

PRINCE.

[*Who has stopped short.*] Well—damn his impudence!

BEAU.

[*Affects not to hear or understand* SHERRY.] I beg your
pardon, who did you say? I had no idea he looked like
that. Is it really? You don't say so? Dear, dear, what
a pity! What a pity!

[*Takes* SHERIDAN'S *arm and they go off at the*
right, BEAU *with his usual imperturbable air*
and SHERIDAN *visibly shaking and dejected.*
The PRINCE *and* MRS. ST. AUBYN *are at the*
left, the PRINCE *speechless with rage and*
MRS. ST. AUBYN *trying to say something*
consoling.]

DUCHESS.

Well, I've had all my pains for nothing.

LADY FARTHINGALE.

But, Duchess, did you see?

DUCHESS.

See what? There was nothing to see! [*With a chuckle.*]
Lud, Beau got the best of it.

MRS. ST. AUBYN.

Duchess, you look ill. Doesn't the air agree with you, or
is it the daylight?

DUCHESS.

[*Loftily.*] I hope, my dear Mrs. St. Aubyn, you'll never
look worse.   [*With a deep curtsy.*]

" Sherry, who's your fat friend ?"

BEAU BRUMMEL

MRS. ST. AUBYN.

[*With affected horror.*] Heaven forbid!

[*The* PRINCE *and* MRS. ST. AUBYN *exit at left.
All the people at back exit.*]

DUCHESS.

Come, let's be going. [LORD MANLY *offers one arm to
the* DUCHESS, LADY FARTHINGALE *takes his other arm.
They move off toward the left.*] Where can Beau have disappeared to? Of course, it's of no interest to us, only I
must say it was uncommonly ill-natured of him not to
make more of a scene for our sakes, you know.

[*They all go out.* BEAU *and* SHERRY *enter
from the right, followed by the two bailiffs.*
SHERIDAN *speaks as they come on.*]

SHERIDAN.

Your marriage, my dear Beau, will redeem your mis-
fortune, and it is the only thing that will.

[*They have reached the center by this time, and*
BEAU *sees the bailiffs. He stops, puts up his
glass, looks at them, and says:*]

BEAU.

[*Shaking his finger at* SHERRY.] Sherry, Sherry, who are
these fellows following you?

[SHERRY *turns and sees the bailiffs and becomes
much agitated.*]

BAILIFF.

Mr. Brummel, sir!

[BEAU *sees it's no use to try to deceive* SHERRY.]

BEAU.

Zounds! Proceed. Sherry, I will join you in a moment.
Well, my good men!

[SHERRY *hurries off, shaking his head sadly.*]

[107]

BEAU BRUMMEL

BEAU.

You donkeys, would you ruin me?

BAILIFF.

Come, come, we've had enough of your airs, now.
You'd better come along with us quietly.

[*Places finger on* BEAU'S *shoulder.*]

BEAU.

[*Moves away.*] For Heaven's sake, don't put those hands
on me! Why don't you wear gloves? [*Bailiff, who had
retreated a step, comes closer.*] And don't come so close.
You are too hasty and ill-advised—you have no manners.
[*Bailiffs retreat in real confusion and astonishment.*]
There's one resource, I must tell them. [*He takes out snuff-
box and takes snuff with great deliberation, and does not
speak until he has returned box, brushed his lace ruffles,
then he turns to them.*] Had you met my valet he would
have delivered to you my message. It was to the effect that
the banns of marriage between the daughter of Mr. Oliver
Vincent and myself are to be published in St. James's on
Sunday. As the son-in-law of the merchant prince I can
not only satisfy your master's demands, but handsomely
remember you yourselves. Now, trot away, trot away,
anywhere out of my sight. [*Turns away.*]

BAILIFF.

We've heard one of your fine stories before, and we
don't go till you prove what you say.

BEAU.

How very annoying! [*Looks off at left and sees* MARIANA.
His face lights up.] Here comes Mariana. Here is the
young lady herself. Withdraw and you shall have your
proof. [*Bailiffs look at each other.*]

FIRST BAILIFF.

[*A little doubtfully.*] Well!

[108]

BEAU BRUMMEL

SECOND BAILIFF.

[*Still more doubtfully.*] Well!!

FIRST BAILIFF.

Well, we'll see what it is, eh?

> [*They exit at the back left. BEAU walks down to the right, brushes his shoulder where bailiff's hand had rested, turns and crosses toward left as though to meet MARIANA, suddenly stops.*]

BEAU.

What! [*Looks again as though he thought himself mistaken.*] Reginald and Mariana! Mariana and Reginald!

> [*Shakes his head as though to dispel the thoughts that would come. Then walks slowly toward the path at back, leading off to the left. MARIANA enters hastily, followed by REGINALD, both much agitated.*]

REGINALD.

I have been wretched beyond the telling—my letters left unanswered, not one word from you in fourteen days.

MARIANA.

My letters and appeals unanswered is what you mean, sir. I wrote you even up to yesterday, and Kathleen vowed that she delivered all the notes till then.

REGINALD.

To whom did she deliver them? 'Twas not to me.

MARIANA.

[*With a cry of joy.*] What, you did not receive them? Then Kathleen has played me false. Oh, Reginald, what I have suffered in wrongly thinking you untrue to me.

REGINALD.

Such doubt of me was cruel, Mariana, but [*lightly*]

BEAU BRUMMEL

come, ask my pardon and see how quickly I'll forgive you.

> [*Comes to her and tries to take her hands, but* MARIANA *draws away.*]

MARIANA.
No—no. I cannot, I cannot.

REGINALD.
[*Misunderstanding.*] Then see, I'll forgive without the asking.

MARIANA.
[*Still refusing to let him take her hand.*] Reginald, what will you think? How can I tell you? It is too late now.

REGINALD.
Too late! What do you mean?

MARIANA.
I have promised myself to another.

> [BEAU *is seen at back, head bowed, attitude one of utter sadness.*]

REGINALD.
[*Forcibly.*] You must break that promise. To whom has it been given?

MARIANA.
To Mr. Brummel.

REGINALD.
Mr. Brummel! [*In shocked surprise.*] Great heavens! Mariana, he is my best friend—my benefactor.

MARIANA.
No—no!

REGINALD.
My mother's only brother. It is he who since her death has cared for me most tenderly and all my life has shielded me from every harm.

BEAU BRUMMEL

Mariana.

He is overwhelmed now by his difficulties. His creditors are like bloodhounds on his track. He has sacrificed himself for me in defence of my father. Through me alone can he be rid of his distresses.

Reginald.

And he loves you. I know that, too, and you, do you love him?

Mariana.

[*Reproachfully.*] You should not ask me that.

Reginald.

[*Taking her hands.*] You are right! But I cannot give you up, nor can I see my uncle ruined; he is the one man in the universe from whom I would not steal your love. 'Tis you who must decide.

Mariana.

And I have done so. I am his.

> [Beau *comes down to the center.* Reginald *and*
> Mariana *draw back on each side.*]

Beau.

No—no, I give you up; I release you from your promise.
> [*The bailiffs enter and stand at back listening.*]

Mariana.

[*Starting forward.*] Sir!

Beau.

Take her, Reginald!
> [*He holds out his hand to* Mariana, *who is
> about to give him hers, when she stops, with-
> draws her hand.*]

Mariana.

No, I am yours. I will not be released. Our love would

[111]

not be happiness if it entailed your ruin. Reginald has told me that he owes to you his life. My father and myself have greater cause for gratitude to you than I can say. I hold you to your vows.

BEAU.
Impossible; I now release you.

REGINALD.
[*Sees the bailiffs.*] Great heavens, the bailiffs! You shall not sacrifice yourself for us. I join with Mariana against myself and say that she is yours.

BEAU.
[*Looks at him with great affection.*] No—no! [*Brushes an imaginary speck from his sleeve.*] I love you both too well to come between your young hearts' happiness.

MARIANA.
[*In a last effort to change him.*] And yet you loved me!
  [BEAU *takes a step toward her with a look of love and reproach.*]

BEAU.
Mariana! No, [*lifting his hat and turning away*] I must leave you.

REGINALD.
You shall not; we will speak to Mr. Vincent and he will help you.

BEAU.
[*Reprovingly.*] I have no claim whatever on Mr. Vincent. [*Bailiffs standing at back give a nod to each other.*] Take her, Reginald; wear her very near your heart for my sake. [*Hands* MARIANA *to* REGINALD.] And now I would accompany you further, but I cannot—not now, [*with a slight, almost imperceptible turn toward the bailiffs*] I happen

*" I happen to have a very pressing engagement
with—with His Majesty."*

to have a very pressing engagement—with—with—His Majesty!

> [BEAU *turns, after a very ceremonious bow to* MARIANA *to the right, and moves off. The bailiffs have come down and follow him closely; one of them taps him on the shoulder.* BEAU *stops for an instant, then takes out snuff-box, and takes snuff and walks slowly off with the greatest dignity.* MARIANA *hides her face on* REGINALD'S *shoulder as curtain comes down.*]

THE END OF THE THIRD ACT

THE FOURTH ACT

SCENE ONE

THE FOURTH ACT
SCENE ONE

A lodging house at Calais—a room at the top of the house. The shabbiest furniture—bare floor—window at the back with rude settle in it; the tops of neighboring houses can be seen from the window. A large fireplace with small fire is at the right, with a door below leading into another room. A table stands in the middle of room with a chair each side. Another door at the left leads into the hall. BEAU is discovered sitting in front of fireplace with his back to the audience. He is dressed in a yellow brocaded dressing-gown, apparently the same one worn in Act I, but with its glory gone, faded and worn, torn in places; he wears old black slippers, with white stockings and brown trousers, "slit so at the bottom and then buttoned tight." His hair is a little gray, his face thin and worn. At rise of curtain MORTIMER enters from hallway. He, too, shows the wear and tear of poverty. All his jauntiness has gone; he is shabbily dressed. After waiting a minute to see if BEAU will notice him he speaks:

MORTIMER

Not a letter, sir. No answer to those we sent over a month ago. Only one to me from Kathleen, to say if I

BEAU BRUMMEL

don't return immediately she will take to Mr. Sheridan's
gentleman for good, and enclosing me the passage money
over. [BEAU *turns a little and looks at him as though to
see if he is going.*] I—I—gave it to the bootmaker, whom
I met at the foot of the stairs with a bailiff as I came in.

> [BEAU *sinks back in his chair again, satisfied
> that* MORTIMER *will not leave him.*]

BEAU.

If you would not use it for yourself, Mortimer, you might
at least have bought a paté for dinner instead; we should
have had something to eat, and we could have made the
bailiff stop and dine with us.   Could you make no further
loans?   [*His voice is harsh and strained.*]

MORTIMER.

No more, sir. I tried everywhere. No one will trust us
any more.

BEAU.

Mortimer, what will become of us? Think what the
finest gentleman of his time is undergoing. It's enough
to drive one mad.

MORTIMER.

Have you nothing more to sell, sir?

> [BEAU *rises and comes to the table. He has
> a snuff-box in his hand; a small black one,
> in great contrast to the jewelled box he carried
> in the earlier scenes.*]

BEAU.

My last snuff-box. You would not have me dispose of
that, Mortimer, a paltry trifle that would bring nothing.
No, there is nothing, Mortimer. Everything belongs to
that wretched female creature who dignifies this hovel
with the name of lodgings.

> [*Loud knocking is heard at the door, which is
> thrown violently open, and the landlady*]

BEAU BRUMMEL

*stalks in.   She is a very determined-looking woman, short
and stout, with a red face and a pronounced
mustache.   She is dressed in a rather short
blue skirt, heavy shoes, blue denim apron,
black blouse with white neckerchief, a white
cap with broad frill.   Stands with arms
akimbo looking at* BEAU *disdainfully.*]

BEAU.
Talking of angels!   Good morning, my dear madam.
So courteous of you to come.   It is not my reception day,
but you are always welcome.   Mortimer, offer this good
lady a chair.

LANDLADY.
[*Speaks with French accent.*]   Chair, humph!   Your
Mortimer had better offer me some money, some rent
money, or I'll have you both shown to the door, do you
hear?   [*Rapping on table,* BEAU *starts as though in
distress at each loud rap.*]   That's what I come to say.
[MORTIMER *now offers her a chair.*]   No, I thank you,
I'll stand!   It's my own chair, and I will not wear it out
by sitting in it.

BEAU.
Then sit in it yourself, Mortimer; I cannot permit you
to stand; you are tired.   I'm so sorry, my dear madam,
that I have nothing to offer you; the supplies for which
Mortimer went out a short time ago have not yet arrived.

LANDLADY.
[*Sneeringly.*]   Supplies!   Not yet arrived!   Well, when
they do they will not pass my door, I'll tell you that.
[*Hammers on table again.*]

BEAU.
[*Wincing.*]   Do, my dear madam, do help yourself.
And speaking of helping yourself reminds me, would you

[119]

mind returning some of my shirts? I am sure you cannot wear them yourself. Mortimer!

MORTIMER.
Yes sir.

BEAU.
How many were there in the wash last week?

MORTIMER.
Twelve, sir.

BEAU.
Yes—now if you wouldn't mind returning—— Mortimer!

MORTIMER.
Yes, sir.

BEAU.
How many shall I require for the remainder of the week?

MORTIMER.
Five, sir.

BEAU.
Yes, if you would not mind returning five, I think I might manage for the remainder of the week.

LANDLADY.
[*Who has been restraining her wrath with difficulty.*] I'll do nothing of the sort, sir, and I'm sick of your fine manners. I want more of the money, and less of the politeness.

[*With an exaggerated bow, mocking* BEAU.]

BEAU.
[*Taking snuff.*] You mean, my dear madam, you want more of the politeness and less of the money.

LANDLADY.
[*Furiously.*] What! You dare insult me? Pay me to-day, or out into the street you go. Your polite talk may

BEAU BRUMMEL

do good there. It may do for the stones, but it will not do for the flesh, not for this flesh. Pauper! Pauper! Bah!

> [*Shouts the last three words and as she gets to the door on "Bah," bangs door and goes out. At the word "Pauper" BEAU stands as though turned to stone.*]

BEAU.

[*Very slowly.*] Mortimer.

MORTIMER.

Yes, sir.

BEAU.

What did she call me?

MORTIMER.

[*Half sobbingly.*] Pauper, sir.

BEAU.

[*Sinking into chair by right of table.*] Pauper!

MORTIMER.

I am afraid, sir, she's in earnest.

BEAU.

[*Quite simply.*] She had that appearance. Mortimer, we must find the money somehow, or I must leave Calais to-night.

MORTIMER.

[*Hesitatingly.*] That packet of letters, sir, for which you have had so many offers from publishers.

BEAU.

What packet, Mortimer?

MORTIMER.

Your private letters of gossip and scandal from people of the Court. I know you have been averse, sir—— [*His voice dies away, as* BEAU, *drawing himself up, gives him a withering glance.*]

[121]

BEAU BRUMMEL

BEAU.

Mortimer, you surprise me. I thought you knew me better. No. I would rather suffer anything than live by sacrificing the reputation of those who once befriended me. [*Opens drawer in table and takes out packet of letters tied with a faded ribbon. Fondles them for an instant, then goes to fireplace, kneels and throws them into the flames.*] There they go, Mortimer. There they go—and almost any one of them might break a heart or blast a reputation, and see how swiftly they vanish, as swiftly as would the reputations which they are destroyed to save.

MORTIMER.

I was wondering, sir, if it would do to appeal to His Majesty. He might overlook what happened when he was Prince. He passes through Calais to-day, sir.

BEAU.

[*Rising and coming to table.*] I have thought of it, Mortimer, but I fear it would be in vain—well, we might try. Go to him, Mortimer, go to him, and take him [*pauses to think what* MORTIMER *can take, and feels snuff-box in pocket, takes it out and handles it lovingly*]—take him this snuff-box. [*Gives* MORTIMER *the box. Hardly has it left his hands, however, when he reaches out for it again.*] That is, you might take him the box, but, perhaps, you'd better not take him the snuff. [MORTIMER *gives* BEAU *the box.* BEAU *picks up a paper lying on the table, saying:*] Bills, bills. [*Makes the paper into a cornucopia, empties the snuff from the box into it, then taps box on the table, loosens any remaining particles of snuff with his finger, then looks at table and scrapes any snuff remaining there into the cornucopia, then hands box to* MORTIMER.] Give it to him with your own hands, say Mr. Brummel presents his compliments. And if that fails, like everything else—why then——

MORTIMER.

And what then, sir?

BEAU BRUMMEL

BEAU.

Then, [*taking snuff elegantly from cornucopia*] then, Mortimer, I can starve. And I promise you I shall do it in the most elegant manner. And you—you, Mortimer, must return to that Japanese girl; what's her name?

MORTIMER.

[*Tearfully.*] Kathleen, sir.

BEAU.

Yes. Kathleen.
> [*Knock at door.* MORTIMER *opens it. Starts back astounded.*]

MORTIMER.

Mr. Vincent, sir.
> [VINCENT *enters puffing from the climb upstairs.*]

BEAU.

[*Is astonished and annoyed, puts the cornucopia of snuff hastily into his pocket, draws his dressing gown around him*]. Mr. Vincent! My dear sir! Why, how did you find your way here? You should have been shown into the reception room, or my drawing-room, or my library; you find me in my morning gown, in my morning room. I make a thousand apologies.

VINCENT.

Don't, don't; I was passing through Calais and I just happened in. Phew, you're pretty high up here.

BEAU.

Yes; the air is so very much purer. Will you be seated Mr. —— It is still *Mr.* Vincent, is it not? [*To himself.*] He must not know my want, my poverty; I could not suffer this man's pity or compassion.

VINCENT.

[*Sits at left of table.*] Before I forget it, let me ask you to do me the honor of dining with me to-day.

[123]

BEAU BRUMMEL

BEAU.

[*With an involuntary drawing in of the breath.*] Dine!
At what hour?

VINCENT.

I always dine at five o'clock.

BEAU.

Thank you; but I fear you will have to excuse me. I
could not possibly dine at such an hour.
[*Turns from table and goes up toward window.*]

VINCENT.

[*Aside.*] Not changed much in spirit, but in everything
else—— [*Aloud.*] Well, Mr. Brummel, you must lead a
dull life of it here in Calais.

BEAU.

[*Still at window and jauntily.*] You forget, Mr. Vincent,
that by living in Calais I do what all the young bucks do—
I pass all my time between London and Paris.

VINCENT.

Witty as ever, Mr. Brummel. The sea air does not
dampen your spirits.

BEAU.

No; and I use none other. That is the reason I have
nothing to offer you. Had I known of your coming I
should have been better prepared to receive you.
[*Comes down and sits at right of table.*]

VINCENT.

[*Looking around the room.*] You must be hard pressed
for money, if you don't mind my saying so.

BEAU.

[*Very hastily and airily, and rising.*] Oh, no! You
have quite a mistaken notion of my affairs, because you
miss certain useless articles given away as pledges——

BEAU BRUMMEL

[*Swallows a word*] ahem—of gratitude for favors shown me. I always pay a debt, Mr. Vincent, when it's a social one.

VINCENT.

But those other debts which rumor says are overwhelming you again. Now if you'd let me pay them——

BEAU.

[*Sits at right of table. In a very cold tone.*] Thank you, thank you. No doubt you intend to be kind, but you are impertinent. [VINCENT *turns away rebuffed and disappointed.* BEAU *to himself*:] No, I will not be so humiliated by *her* father. I would rather tell a little lie instead. [*To* VINCENT.] I assure you, since the renewal of my friendship with the Prince, now His Majesty!——

[*Makes a slight bow at "His Majesty."*]

VINCENT.

[*Coming down, delighted.*] Friendship with His Majesty!

BEAU.

What! Has not rumor told you that, too? She's a sorry jade, and sees only the gloomy side of things. Then, I suppose you have not heard that the King has pensioned me! [*Takes handkerchief from pocket; it is full of holes.*]

VINCENT.

But——

BEAU.

I see you still have that very unfortunate habit of "butting." Why how, how, without a pension could I keep up this establishment? [*Holding up the tattered handkerchief in his trembling hand, he says, aside:*] If he can tell me that he will help me more than he knows.

VINCENT.

All the more reason, then, why you should return to London and marry my daughter.

[125]

BEAU BRUMMEL

BEAU.

Are you still obstinate on that point? Do you still refuse her to Reginald? [*Knock is heard at door.*]

VINCENT.

There is Mariana. I told her to join me here.

BEAU.

[*Rises in consternation, draws his dressing gown around him, looks down at it.*] Mariana—Miss Vincent, coming here. Mr. Vincent, one moment, one moment, Mr. Vincent, one moment.

        [*Goes hastily to door at right, bows to* VINCENT *and exits.* MARIANA *enters from hall door at left.*]

MARIANA.

Is he here? Have you succeeded?

VINCENT.

My child, we have heard false reports in town. He has a pension from His Majesty. He is friends with the King. Dear me! I hope I haven't offended him.

MARIANA.

A pension, papa! [*And then as she looks around the dingy room.*] Are you quite sure he's not deceiving you?

VINCENT.

Quite sure, he could not deceive me.

MARIANA.

Then, father, there is no further need for me to make the sacrifice you demanded, and which Mr. Brummel's need did justify.

VINCENT.

By no means. I am all the more determined on it.

MARIANA.

I also am determined now, and say I will not marry him.

[126]

BEAU BRUMMEL

VINCENT.

Tut, tut! Hush, he's coming—he's somewhat changed.

[BEAU *enters. He has put on his coat—a shabby, full-skirted brown coat. Has dingy black neckerchief on. Bows very low to* MARIANA.]

BEAU.

Good morning, my dear Miss Vincent. I trust the stairs have not fatigued you; you should feel at home, so high up among the angels.

MARIANA.

[*Shows she is much affected by* BEAU'S *changed appearance.*] I am most pleased, sir, that we find you happy with the world and with yourself. We had feared otherwise.

BEAU.

I lead a charmed life; even now, you see, it brings you to me.

MARIANA.

And has it brought your nephew, too, sir?

BEAU.

That may be your privilege.

MARIANA.

I trust it may be, or else that you will bring him back to me.

[*As she says this she turns away and goes up toward the window with* VINCENT, *who shows he is not pleased at this speech. At this moment* REGINALD *rushes in, throwing hat on table as he goes by, and rushing up to* BEAU, *holds out his hand eagerly.*]

REGINALD.

Uncle!

[127]

BEAU BRUMMEL

BEAU.

[*With great affection.*] Reginald! [*Then recollecting himself.*] No, Reginald, a glance of the eye. Reginald, my boy, you here, too!

REGINALD.

I heard yesterday of your distresses——

BEAU.

[*Hastily interrupting him.*] Do you not see Miss Vincent and her father? [REGINALD *turns, sees* MARIANA *and crosses to window to her, where they stand eagerly talking.* VINCENT *goes toward hall door, evidently very anxious to get* MARIANA *away.*] I might have accepted it from him, but he has come too late. This Vincent shall not know the truth. But Reginald shall have Mariana and Vincent shall give her to him.

VINCENT.

I think, my dear, you had better go and wait down stairs for me.

BEAU.

No, no, let Miss Vincent remain; my nephew will entertain her, [REGINALD *and* MARIANA *at this begin talking more confidentially*] and I wish to consult you privately in my room for a few moments.

VINCENT.

Now, my dear Mr. Brummel, I must insist on Mariana's retiring.

BEAU.

And I must insist that Miss Vincent remain. I see your manners have not improved. I will not detain you a moment. I wish to ask your advice. I hear an earldom is soon likely to become vacant. Now, who's eligible?

VINCENT.

An earldom!

[128]

BEAU BRUMMEL

B E A U .

You know more about matters in town than I, and I wish to be prepared in case my influence should be needed. Now what name would you suggest?

V I N C E N T .

[*Gasping.*] You honor me, Mr. Brummel.

B E A U .

Very likely, but I wish you wouldn't gasp so. Indeed, I do honor you in asking you for your daughter's hand——
> [REGINALD *and* MARIANA *start and look around.*]

V I N C E N T .

[*Bows very low.*] Mr. Brummel!

B E A U .

For my nephew!
> [REGINALD *and* MARIANA *turn again toward window relieved.*]

V I N C E N T .

My dear Mr. Brummel, you know I am opposed to that, and I hope to persuade you——

B E A U .

[*Significantly.*] Who is eligible for the earldom—exactly—and I think—mind, I say, I think—we both have the same person in mind. But, first, I must persuade you who is eligible for your daughter.
> [*He bows to* VINCENT *and motions him to door at right.*]

V I N C E N T .

[*Speaking as he goes.*] Gad! Zounds! An earldom! If this should be my opportunity at last. Mariana *shall* marry the boy if he wants it.   [*Exits.*]

BEAU BRUMMEL

BEAU.

[*Turns to speak to* MARIANA *and* REGINALD *and finds them so absorbed in each other they do not even see him. He attracts their attention by knocking a chair on the floor. They start guiltily apart.*] My dears, I am about to draw up the marriage settlement, and, perhaps, I'll make my will at the same time and leave you everything. [*They both bow.*] I will now allow you to settle the preliminaries by yourselves.

> [*They immediately retire again to the window and are once more absorbed in each other.* BEAU *stands watching them for a few minutes, then turns away, puts hand over his eyes and totters off.*]

MARIANA.

[*Coming down left of table.*] But I don't understand, do you?

REGINALD.

[*Coming down to her side.*] I don't desire to. I take the fact as it is. [*Kisses her.*]

MARIANA.

I think you take much else besides, sir. Aren't you a trifle precipitate?

REGINALD.

No, this is the first preliminary. [*Puts arm around her waist.*] I think I shall linger over the preliminaries.

MARIANA.

But has my father relented?

REGINALD.

Surely! Or why did you come here?

MARIANA.

We heard Mr. Brummel was in great distress and we came to help him, but we found the rumors were false; his friendship with the King has been renewed.

[130]

*"We found the rumors were false; his friendship with
the King has been renewed."*

BEAU BRUMMEL

REGINALD.

Thank Heaven! Then his troubles are at an end.

MARIANA.

My father still clung to the idea of our marriage.

REGINALD.

And you?

MARIANA.

That question is superfluous, sir. Have I not allowed the first preliminaries to be settled.

> [BEAU *and* VINCENT *enter*—VINCENT *a little ahead of* BEAU. *Also* MORTIMER *comes on dejectedly from hall door.*]

BEAU.

Reginald, give me your hand. [REGINALD *crosses to him.*]

VINCENT.

[*Who has crossed over to left of table.*] Mariana, come to your father. Are you still bent on marrying him?

MARIANA.

You mean, papa, that he is still bent on marrying me, and that I—I am not unwilling.

VINCENT.

She is yours, sir.

REGINALD.

[*Coming back to* MARIANA.] Mine!

MORTIMER.

[*Goes up to* BEAU *at right of table and hands him snuff-box.*] It was returned without a word, sir

BEAU.

[*In a loud tone.*] Beg Her Grace to excuse me this afternoon.

MORTIMER.

Yes, sir.

REGINALD.

You will dine with us, Uncle Beau, on board the vessel?

[131]

BEAU BRUMMEL

BEAU.

Thank you, but I fear you will have to excuse me, and now pardon me if I ask you to retire. I happen to have a very pressing engagement.

MARIANA.

When will you be in London, sir. You will be there for our wedding?

BEAU.

I hope so—and you must accept some little present, some little trifle, some little token of my affection and regard—some—some—remembrance. Now what shall it be? Eh? What shall we say? [*They all look around the room, which is, of course, bare of all ornament.*] What do you really think you would like best—hum? [*Absently fingers the snuff-box which* MORTIMER *brought him.*] Ah, yes, this snuff-box—it has just been sent to me by—His Majesty.

[*Hands* MARIANA *snuff-box, which she takes with deep curtsy and goes back to* REGINALD, *showing it to him.*]

VINCENT.

[*At door as he goes out.*] I shall probably hear from you, Mr. Brummel?

BEAU.

[*Absently.*] Ah, yes, perhaps—good-by. Reginald, [REGINALD *comes to him,* BEAU *places his hand on* REGINALD'S *shoulder*] God bless you——

[REGINALD *picks up hat from table and crosses to door.* MARIANA *comes down, gives hand to* BEAU, *curtsies,* BEAU *raises hand to his lips.* MARIANA *draws it away, backs toward door, makes another curtsy, turns to* REGINALD *and they go off gaily, apparently talking to each other.* BEAU *puts hand over eyes, staggers back and leans against table for support.*]

CURTAIN FALLS ON THIS.

[132]

THE FOURTH ACT

SCENE TWO

BEAU BRUMMEL
THE FOURTH ACT
SCENE TWO

*An attic room. Sloping roof. Walls discolored with the
damp. Paper peeling off. Window at the back. A bare
deal table over near the left with one chair at its side.
Another chair stands down near the front at the right-
hand side. Another chair stands at the back near window. There is a door at the right and also at the left.*

> [BEAU *enters at the right hand door. You can
> hear him for some time before he enters
> stumbling up the stairs as though feeble.
> He stands for a moment at the door, bowing
> very low. He is very shabbily dressed—his
> hat battered—his boots gray.*]

BEAU.

I thought I saw the Prince there, [*pointing to chair*]
there! The boys mocked me in the streets—they threw
stones at me. No wonder; there has been no varnish on my
boots for days. They refused to give me a cup of coffee
or a macaroon. They would rather see me starve—and
starve so in rags. [*Sits in chair.*]

MORTIMER.

[*Enters from door at left.*] Shall I announce dinner, sir?

BEAU.

[*Starting.*] No, Mortimer, I have only just come in, and
you forget this is Thursday, when I always entertain.
[*Sinks into a reverie.*]

MORTIMER.

Poor Mr. Brummel! He's getting worse and worse.
Lack of food is turning his head instead of his stomach.
But I don't dare oppose him when he's this way.

BEAU.

Mortimer!

[135]

BEAU BRUMMEL

MORTIMER.

Yes, sir.

BEAU.

I could get nothing for us to eat, Mortimer, nothing—
and they refused to wash my cravats!

MORTIMER.

Oh, Mr. Brummel, sir, what shall we do? We will
starve, sir.

BEAU.

[*Severely.*] Mortimer, you forget yourself! Who has
called during my absence?

MORTIMER.

[*Goes up to the window ledge and brings down an old
broken plate with a few dirty cards.*] These cards won't
last much longer. I have been bringing him the same ones
on Thursday for the last year. [BEAU *has fallen asleep.*]
Mr. Brummel, sir! Mr. Brummel, sir!
            [*He puts plate directly in front of* BEAU.]

BEAU.

[BEAU *starts—looks at plate.*] The—the—card tray.

MORTIMER.

We've—lent it, sir!
            [*He pushes cards forward with his thumb and
            finger as* BEAU *takes them one by one and
            lays them back on plate.*]

BEAU.

Duchess of Leamington—thank goodness, I was out.
Lord Manly—do we owe him anything?

MORTIMER.

No, sir.

BEAU.

Why not? Mrs. St. Aubyn—and I missed her—no
matter. They will all dine here this evening.

BEAU BRUMMEL

MORTIMER.

[*Taking plate back to ledge.*] Dine—that's the way we eat—the names of things—but it is very weakening—very weakening.

BEAU.

Mortimer!

MORTIMER.

Yes, sir.

BEAU.

Light the candelabra. [*Begins to sing very low in a quavering voice*:] "She Wore a Wreath of Roses."

MORTIMER.

Yes, sir. [*He goes to window ledge and brings down to table two pewter candlesticks with a little piece of a candle in each one. He lights both and then with a quick look at* BEAU *blows out one.*] He'll never know, and if it burns there will be none to light the next time.

BEAU.

Mortimer!

MORTIMER.

Yes, sir.

BEAU.

Is my hat on?

MORTIMER.

[*Choking back a sob.*] Yes, sir.

BEAU.

[*Lifts hat with elegant gesture, his hand drops and hat falls to the floor, rises.*] Mortimer, I hear carriage wheels— carriage wheels! Observe me, Mortimer, am I quite correct? Are there creases in my cravat! I would not wish to make creases the fashion.

MORTIMER.

Mr. Brummel, sir, you are quite correct.

[137]

BEAU BRUMMEL

BEAU.

To your post. Bid the musicians play. [*Bows as though welcoming guest.*] Ah, Duchess, you are always welcome! And in pink! You come like the rosy morning sunshine into the darkness of my poor lodgings. Lord Manly! And sober —truth is stranger than fiction. The Duchess's smiles should have intoxicated you. Mrs. St. Aubyn—Your Majesty! [*Bows very low.*] Pray, sir, honor my poor arm. Permit me to conduct Your Majesty to a chair whilst I receive my less distinguished guests. [*Walks to chair with imaginary guest on his arm.*] My dear Lady Farthingale, how do you do? As beautiful and as charming as ever. [*Backs up a little and kicks a chair over.*] I beg ten thousand pardons! My dear Lady Cecilie, how you have grown and how beautiful. [*With vacant stare.*] Shall we dine? Dine! Shall we dine? Permit me to escort Your Majesty to the table where we dine! [*Goes to chair and escorts the imaginary king to the table.*] Yours is the honor and mine, Lady Cecilie, my charming *vis-à-vis*. Mariana—Mariana—always nearest my heart—always. Mortimer—Mortimer!

MORTIMER.

[*Who has been leaning against the wall with head on arm.*] Yes, sir.

BEAU

His Majesty waits! [*Bows to right and left.*] Enchanted! Enchanted! [*Waits until, apparently, they are all seated and then sits.*] I trust you will find these oysters agreeable; they arrived but this morning from Ostend. Bird's-nest soup. It is very hot. I am very particular to have the soup hot on these cold evenings. This is very good melon.

MORTIMER.

[*Who has been pretending to pass things.*] Melon, sir.

BEAU.

Duchess, I trust you are fond of ortolans stuffed with

[138]

truffles. Brown—and glazed. My chef—my chef——
[*Voice dies away.*]

MORTIMER.

His chef! If only we had something to cook, I should
not mind the chef.   [*Sinks in chair.*]

BEAU.

Mariana, let me fill your glass and drink with me. My
dear. My own always. My only dear one.

[*Head sinks on chest, he falls asleep.*]

KATHLEEN.

[*After a pause* KATHLEEN *puts her head in the
door and says very softly:*]

And may I come in?

MORTIMER.

[*Rising in bewilderment.*] Kathleen! And has it gone to
my head, too?

KATHLEEN.

[*Half crying.*] No, but to my heart!—or to yours—for
they've gotten that mixed I don't know which is which.

[*They embrace.*]

MORTIMER.

[*In alarm, fearing* BEAU *may wake.*] Hush!

KATHLEEN.

Miss Mariana that was, Mrs. Reginald Courtenay that
is, is out in the hall and him with her.

[MARIANA *and* REGINALD *come in at door.*]

MARIANA.

Is he here?

[*Gives a low, horrified exclamation at* BEAU'S
changed appearance.]

MORTIMER.

Yes, madam, but I fear the sudden surprise of seeing
you will kill him.

BEAU BRUMMEL

REGINALD.

But the King is in town with his suite. We came with him, and they followed us here immediately.

MORTIMER.

The King!

MARIANA.

Yes, Mortimer; your master's and your troubles are over.

[MARIANA *and* REGINALD *cross to other side of table, away from door.*]

KATHLEEN.

[*Aside to* MORTIMER, *as she goes up to window.*] I am not so sure but yours are just beginning.

KING.

[*Appearing at door.*] Zounds—is this——

MORTIMER.

[*Bowing very low.*] Your Majesty, I beg your pardon, but—sh—sh——

MRS. ST. AUBYN.

[*At door.*] Dear me, you don't——

KING.

[*Turning to her.*] Sh—sh——

DUCHESS.

But how——

KING.

[KING *goes through same pantomime, turning, putting finger on lip and saying* :]

Sh!

LADY FARTHINGALE.

Where is Mr. Brummel?

KING.

[*As before.*] Sh! Sh!

[140]

" Your master's and your troubles are over."

BEAU BRUMMEL

LORD MANLY.

Well——

KING.

[*As before.*] Sh! Sh!

MORTIMER.

If Your Majesty will pardon me, I think I could suggest something. Mr. Brummel has just been imagining you were all dining with him. I think if you were to take your places at the table, when he saw you the truth would gradually come to him.

[*They all sit.* KING *at left,* MRS. ST. AUBYN *next, then the* DUCHESS. MARIANA *and* REGINALD *are at the right.*]

MORTIMER.

Mr. Brummel! [*Louder, as* BEAU *does not move.*] Mr. Brummel, sir!

BEAU.

Duchess, let me send you this saddle of venison; it's delicious. [*Wakes, looks around, sees* MARIANA.] Mariana! Mariana! Reginald! [*They come to his side.*] Pardon me for not rising; I think I must have forgotten my manners. You won't leave me Mariana? You won't leave me, will you, will you?

MARIANA.

No, Mr. Brummel.

BEAU.

[*Sees* MRS. ST. AUBYN.] Mrs. St. Aubyn, you—you forgive?

MRS. ST. AUBYN.

[*Very gently.*] And forget, Mr. Brummel.

BEAU.

[*Sees the* KING.] Your Majesty! Mortimer!

MORTIMER.

Yes, sir.

[141]

BEAU BRUMMEL

BEAU.

Is this real—is it—is it?

KING.

Yes, Beau, you've hidden from all of us long enough—but now we've found you we don't mean to lose you. We sup with you to-night; to-morrow you dine in London with us.

BEAU.

Dine! [*Drawing in his breath appreciatively.*] Dine—— [*Then remembering.*] At what hour?

MORTIMER.

[*Bowing and whispering to the* KING.] At eight, Your Majesty, at eight!

KING.

[*With a nod of understanding.*] At eight o'clock.

BEAU.

Mortimer, have I any other engagement?

MORTIMER.

[*With fear and trembling.*] No—oh, no, sir!

BEAU.

I shall have much pleasure. Mortimer!

MORTIMER.

Yes, sir.

BEAU.

Mortimer!

MORTIMER.

Yes, sir.

BEAU.

Should anybody call, say I have a very pressing engagement with—with—His Majesty.

[*His head falls, he sinks into chair, supported by* MARIANA *and* REGINALD. *All rise.*]

THE END

[142]

DATE DUE

GAYLORD   PRINTED IN U.S.A.

NOTE

*T*HE idea of this Play was Richard Mansfield's, and the author gratefully acknowledges his debt to the actor for innumerable suggestions.

BEAU BRUMMEL

John and Bimi

July 1960